Apatheia
IN THE CHRISTIAN TRADITION

Apatheia
IN THE CHRISTIAN TRADITION

An Ancient Spirituality
and Its Contemporary Relevance

Joseph H. Nguyen, SJ

CASCADE *Books* • Eugene, Oregon

Cascade Books
An Imprint of Wipf and Stock Publishers
199 W. 8th Ave., Suite 3
Eugene, OR 97401

www.wipfandstock.com

PAPERBACK ISBN: 978-1-5326-4516-7
HARDCOVER ISBN: 978-1-5326-4517-4
EBOOK ISBN: 978-1-5326-4518-1

Cataloguing-in-Publication data:

Names: Nguyen, Joseph H.

Title: Apatheia in the Christian tradition : an ancient spirituality and its contemporary relevance / Joseph H. Nguyen, SJ.

Description: Eugene, OR: Cascade Books, 2018 | Includes bibliographical references.

Identifiers: ISBN 978-1-5326-4516-7 (paperback) | ISBN 978-1-5326-4517-4 (hardcover) | ISBN 978-1-5326-4518-1 (ebook)

Subjects: LCSH: Spiritual life—Christianity—History of doctrines | Spirituality—Christianity | Stoics | Evagrius, Ponticus, 345?–399 | Cassian, John, approximately 360-approximately 435 | Maximus, Confessor, Saint, approximately 580-662 | Ignatius, of Loyola, Saint, 1491–1556 | Asceticism

Classification: BV4501.3 N389 2018 (print) | BV4501.3 (ebook)

Manufactured in the U.S.A.   02/08/18

Contents

Preface

The original insight of the present book comes from my doctoral dissertation entitled, *Transformation and Divine Union: The Concept of Apatheia and "Indifference" in Maximus the Confessor and Ignatius of Loyola—A Comparison*, which I completed at the Jesuit School of Theology at Santa Clara University in the Spring of 2015. It has been more than two years since the time I completed the writing of the dissertation; my thoughts on *apatheia* continue to develop and become more mature. I offer these pages to the readers with the hope that they will awaken a sense of curiosity and appreciation for the continuity and change in the Christian spiritual tradition, particularly in regard to the understanding of *apatheia* in spiritual practice.

I would like to take the opportunity on the completion of the book to thank Dr. Eric Cunningham, Professor of History at Gonzaga University, for his valuable suggestions on how to write a book on a single concept. I would like to thank Wipf and Stock Publishers who accepted my book for publication, in particular the editor, Dr. Robin Parry, for his help editing the book. I would like to thank Dr. Thomas Cattoi, Professor of Christology and Culture at the Jesuit School of Theology at Santa Clara University; Dr. Cattoi served as the director of my doctoral dissertation a few years ago; his interest and knowledge of the spiritual theology of early church has been inspiring for me. The present book would not have been possible without the sound advice, support, and solidarity of my brother Jesuits. I would like to thank John McGarry, SJ, Steve

Preface

Dillard, SJ, Hung Pham, SJ, and Kevin Burke, SJ, professors and staff at the Jesuit School of Theology and the Jesuit Community in Berkeley, California. Many Jesuits with whom I lived, studied, and prayed during my doctoral study in Berkeley are greatly appreciated. Thank you for your friendship and support. Finally, I would like to thank the Della Strada Jesuit Community in Spokane and my colleagues in the Department of Religious Studies at Gonzaga University. Thank you for your friendship and support, without which the present book would not have been possible.

Joseph H. Nguyen, SJ
Gonzaga University, Spokane, Washington
Fall, 2017

Introduction

Human beings have the desire for self-transcendence. From a religious point of view, this desire is often known as the desire to become like the divine, one that presupposes a path that leads to divine union. While the human desire for divine union is a universal phenomenon, each religious tradition offers a distinctive path to that union. In the Christian tradition, this path presupposes a certain theological-anthropological view and a method for spiritual practice and growth.

The Christian theological-anthropological view is grounded in the belief that human beings are created in the image and likeness of God (Gen 1:26).[1] There are two implications that follow from this belief. First, being created in the image of God entails that human beings are endowed with the capability to become like God. In this view, human beings are embodied-spirits, created from matter, but with the very breath of God (Gen 2:7). It is the breath of God, or God's own spirit, that enables human beings towards self-transcendence; and in the Christian spiritual tradition this self-transcendence is realized in the state of divine union, a state where the human spirit is united with the spirit of God. Second, being created in the likeness of God entails that human beings are destined to become like God. God created human beings

1. "Then God said, 'Let us make humankind in our image, according to our likeness; and let them have dominion over the fish of the sea, and over the birds of the air, and over the cattle, and over all the wild animals of the earth, and over every creeping thing that creeps upon the earth'" (Gen 2:26, NRSV). Hereafter all references from the Bible will be taken from the NRSV.

for union with God, and so human beings are not only capable of
divine union, but are also yearning for this union, a yearning that
generates a call, and with it, a destiny, to become like the divine.
This destiny is realized, first, in Jesus Christ, the incarnation of
God, the God who has become human and dwelt among us (John
1:14). The two natures of Jesus Christ, one human and one divine,
are completely united in the Word, the divine Son of God. Second,
by the grace of Christ and through spiritual practice, Christians,
individually and collectively, are called to this life in union with
God in Christ and thus fulfill their destiny as created in the image
and likeness of God.

Grounded in this theological-anthropological point of view,
Christian spiritual theologians throughout the centuries have articulated various pathways to divine union. This book will study
four distinctive but interrelated pathways from four theologians:
Evagrius Ponticus (345–399), John Cassian (360–435), Maximus
the Confessor (580–662), and Ignatius of Loyola (1491–1556).
These four theologians share a common view that a path to divine
union generally consists of three stages commonly known as *practical*, *natural*, and *theological* stages in the Eastern tradition, and
purgative, *illuminative*, and *unitive* stages in the Latin West.

Central to the three stages of spiritual development is the understanding of *apatheia*. In this view, *apatheia* is the condition of
the mind free from disordered bodily senses, disordered emotions,
and disordered attachments to material things and states of life, a
kind of spiritual disposition that comes as a result of a life of prayer
and spiritual discipline.

The early church's view on *apatheia* has its roots in the Stoic
philosophical tradition. Stoic developments of thought can generally be characterized according three periods respectively. The early Stoics lived from the late fourth century to second century BCE,
with Zeno being the founder of the Stoic school of thought and
Chrysippus its prominent thinker. The middle Stoics lived from
the late second century to first century BCE; their thought was
more influenced by Plato, and thus, was considered a divergence
from the early Stoics. The later Stoics consisted mainly of Roman

Introduction

Stoic figures such as Seneca and Marcus Aurelius, who lived in the first and second centuries CE, and whose thought was considered an attempt to retrieve the original thought of the early Stoics. *Apatheia* was a central notion for the Stoics. In exploring the concept of *apatheia*, therefore, one must take into consideration developments in Stoicism, for some early church theologians share similar views, ones that are consistent with the Stoic tradition.

In essence, Stoics are different from Plato in that for them emotions are not mere physiological reactions, but they are mental attitudes and judgments of reality. This view was affirmed by Chrysippus, the prominent thinker of the early Stoics, and was commonly held by the later Stoics, such as Seneca and Marcus Aurelius. By contrast, Plato thinks emotions are caused by bodily sensations and can be irrational and therefore they cannot be mental judgments of reality; rather, he said, emotions ought to be controlled by reason.

In regard to *apatheia*, the Stoics' view is that *apatheia* is the state of the mind free of disordered emotions, *but good emotions remain*. Now Plato did not use the term *apatheia* to describe the state of the mind in tranquility, but in his theory of the human soul he conceives the soul as having three parts: the rational, the irascible, and the sensible. In Plato's view, only the rational part of the soul is capable of mental judgment of reality. While Stoics would insist that *apatheia* is not a non-emotional state of the mind, Plato would conceive *apatheia* as a state of pure intellect, without any emotion. Chapter 1 of the book will discuss the Stoic view on *apatheia*.

The second chapter of the book, in many ways, functions as the transition from the Stoics to the early Christians, with particular regard to the shift in perspective on the nature and function of *apatheia* in spiritual practice. In this regard, Evagrius Ponticus (345–399), a learned monk of the fourth century, was the leading theologian. Evagrius developed a view of spiritual progress in which *apatheia* was a central concept. The chapter will present Evagrius's overall theological anthropology and spiritual practice. Evagrius lived in the fourth century CE; there was a big gap of time and spiritual development between him and the Stoics. Needless to say, Evagrius must have inherited the spiritual developments of theologians who had gone before him, in particular Origen of Alexandria (185–254), whose influence on Evagrius should not be overlooked. Only by making the connection between these early Christian thinkers and the Stoics can the development of the spiritual theology of Evagrius be better understood and appropriated.

Then came John Cassian (360–435), an ascetic who inherited much from the spiritual practices found in the writings of Evagrius. The important role of Cassian in the development of spiritual theology in the West will be discussed in Chapter 3 of the book. Cassian was educated in the Latin language, but was also fluent in Greek, and he travelled in both the Greek-speaking East (Palestine and Egypt) and the Latin-speaking West (France and Italy). Because of his familiarity with both East and West and their theological developments, Cassian became a bridge to connect the two traditions and was also an instrumental translator of the some of the important Eastern ascetical works into Latin. The third chapter of this book will present Cassian's theological anthropology and his understanding of prayer, exploring the continuity and change in Cassian's development of the tradition of *apatheia*.

Chapter 4 will present *apatheia* in the thought of Maximus the Confessor (580–662). Maximus lived in a civilization that valued tradition. Indeed, he himself emphasized the great importance of tradition. In this regard, Maximus inherited his method for scriptural interpretation from Origen and the ascetical tradition from Evagrius Ponticus. But he was probably more influenced by the theology of the Cappadocian fathers, Basil the Great (320–379), Gregory of Nyssa (332–395), and Gregory of Nazianzus (329–389). While Maximus's spiritual theology developed from the ascetical tradition he had inherited from Evagrius Ponticus, it also diverged from Evagrius's in an essential way, in part because of his ability to synthesize the various theological trends that had come before. In doing so, Maximus sought to articulate and select what had been authentic and useful to the understanding of the Christian faith, while he corrected that which he judged had been inconsistent with the faith. As a result, one sees in Maximus a restructuring of the tradition in such a way that seemingly unrelated ideas and insights from the past become interconnected. Chapter 4 of the book will study Maximus's theological anthropology and present his ascetical practice in contradistinction to that of Evagrius Ponticus, particularly with regard to their different views on *apatheia* and divine union.

The final chapter will be dedicated to the study of the mystic who belonged to a completely different era than the first three theologians discussed in the book: Ignatius of Loyola. Ignatius (1491–1556) was born in the Basque country in Northern Spain, into a time of great cultural and religious changes in Europe, that of the late medieval period into the Renaissance of the sixteenth century. Ignatius was the founder of the Society of Jesus, a newly established religious ordered in 1540. Its members are known as the Jesuits. The Jesuit order marked a significant departure from the existing religious orders of the church in the degree to which contemplation and apostolic service were intrinsically bound. This should not be taken to imply that Ignatius's *Spiritual Exercises*, the book composed by Ignatius himself based on his own experiences of God, are not rooted in and consistent with the Christian spiritual tradition. The task of the final chapter is to present and argue for an Ignatian view on *indifferentia*, a Spanish word translated as "indifference" in English. Similar to the Greek term *apatheia*, employed by the ascetical tradition of the early church, Ignatian indifference, too, was rooted in the Stoic tradition, though this connection between Ignatius and the Stoics has not been sufficiently studied and articulated. What are the nature and function of indifference in the *Spiritual Exercises* of Saint Ignatius of Loyola? How do they compare to the nature and function of *apatheia* in the spiritual tradition of the early church? The chapter will address these questions.

The overall aim of the book is three-fold: First, to present the views on *apatheia* and *indifferentia* respectively by tracing their origins to the developments from the Stoic philosophical tradition; Second, to articulate the central theological-anthropological developments and their implications for Christian ascetical practice, represented by Evagrius Ponticus, John Cassian, Maximus the Confessor, and Ignatius of Loyola; Third, to present various methods for prayer and spiritual discernment within the Christian tradition based on the underpinning theological-anthropological developments from the above-mentioned theologians. My hope is that you, the reader, will come to a better understanding and appreciation of the Christian spiritual tradition and appropriate its insights for your own ongoing spiritual practice and growth.

CHAPTER 1

Apatheia in the Stoic Philosophical Tradition

The Greek concept of *apatheia* often has a negative connotation in our time because of its close relation to the English word "apathy," which used to mean "freedom from suffering/passion" and has gradually morphed into meaning "indifference, a lack of interest or motivation." However, in the Stoic philosophical tradition, *apatheia* has a very different meaning from "apathy." In this view, *apatheia* does not imply a state of non-emotion (or a lack of concern). Rather, it connotes the state of "spiritual peace," or the "well-being" of the human soul wherein excessive and negative emotions, such as lust, excessive desire for food and drink, anger, envy, resentment, self-love, and pride are replaced by reasonable desires, love, and humility. In other words, *apatheia* is not a *non-emotional* state, but a state of *healthy* emotions.

The Stoic concept of *apatheia* is grounded in their philosophical and religious view of the world. Central to this view is the belief that human beings are endowed with reason and intellectual will suitable for a life in pursuit of knowledge and virtue, and the attainment of knowledge and virtue becomes the condition for human flourishing. However, the attainment of knowledge and virtue is conditioned by *apatheia*, the healthy state of the human soul. Seen from this perspective, *apatheia* is pivotal to the personal constitution and thus an ideal personal trait. A person who has attained *apatheia* is able to choose and act according to his or her nature, as opposed to a person whose soul is under the influence of disordered desires, whereby the will is not able to decide and act according to its natural condition.

But how does one reach this healthy state of being? The Stoic's method for the attainment of *apatheia* depends upon a particular analysis of the complexity of human emotion. To understand it we must distinguish between external things and our perceptions and judgments of them. External things such material possession, one's state of life, health condition, and profession are considered the factors of life. These factors are external to us in that they *happen to us* and we may or may not have control over them. Whereas our perceptions and judgments of the external facts of life are *internal* to us in that we can observe these factors and cultivate a healthy judgment on them. In Stoic view, the factors of life come and go depending on life circumstances, but they are not constitutive of our moral being and existence. It is our mental judgments and attitudes toward them constitute our characteristic features and personal traits. These features and traits inform and dictate our emotions regarding the external factors of life, and our emotions, in turn, inform and dictate our choices and actions. Our choices and actions manifest our personal characteristics and demonstrate the state of our happiness or unhappiness, whereby happiness means the flourishing of the human life and unhappiness is the contrary state of life.[1]

For Stoics, emotions are not mere physiological reactions to external things but mental perceptions and judgments about them.[2] Emotions are categorized into two types: good (ordered, or healthy) emotions and bad (disordered, or sick) emotions. The goal of spiritual practice is to eradicate *disordered* emotions by transforming them into *healthy* emotions. This transformation

---

1. Hadot, *Philosophy as a Way of Life*, 84.
2. Sorabji, *Emotion and Peace of Mind*, 1–2.

takes place through an educational process that leads to correct judgment and mental attitude toward external reality.

The Greek term for disordered emotion is *pathe*, which is often translated into English as "passion." *Pathe* is the contrary state of *apatheia*. But this English translation of *pathe* can be misleading because the word "passion" often connotes the state of having a strong feeling about doing something; for example, one can have a passion for sports, another can have a passion for arts. In the Christian context, "passion" can also be understood as "the passion of Jesus Christ," referring to Christ's suffering and death. The Stoic *pathe* connotes neither of these meanings.

Stoic *pathe* can be correctly described as an *excessive* emotion that has gone *beyond a reasonable judgment;* nonetheless, it is not an irrational judgment. In his famous work, *On Anger*, Seneca (4 BCE–65 CE), one of the later Stoics, describes the process of how anger, an excessive emotion, develops in a person. It begins with an appearance of what seems to a person to be injustice, to the making of a judgment that it *is* actually an injustice, to the decision to avenge oneself against the offender at all cost. This gradual process involves three different but interrelated movements of anger and their corresponding human reactions:

> In order that you may know how emotions (*edfectus*) (1) begin, or (2) grow, or (3) are carried away (*efferri*), (1) the first movement is involuntary (*nonvoluntarius)* like a preparation for emotion and a kind of threat. (2) The second movement is accompanied by will (*voluntas*), not an obstinate one, to the effect that it is appropriate (*aporteat*) for me to be avenged since he has committed a crime. (3) The third movement is by now uncontrolled (*impotens*), and wills (*vult*) to be avenged, not if it is appropriate (*si oportet*), but come what may (*utique*), and it has overthrown (*evicit*) reason.
>
> (Seneca, *On Anger* 2, 4:1).[3]

According to Seneca, only the second and third movements can properly be called "emotions," while the first movement is

3. Cited by Sorabji, *Emotion and Peace of Mind*, 63.

categorized as a mere physiological shock. Furthermore, there is a difference between the second and third movements. In the second movement, the emotion is appropriate and thus produces an appropriate response; whereas in the case of the third movement, the emotion has become excessive and thus the course of action has gone beyond what is reasonable. In this case, an emotion has become disordered.

Martha Nussbaum translates the Stoic term *pathe* into English as "suffering," emphasizing that it is a passive state of *being done to*, rather than the active state of *doing*.[4] In her view, a person under disordered emotions is a sick person. He or she cannot live according to the capacity of making choices and actions according to reason and rational will. For this reason, a person under the influence of the passions needs to be healed of their sickness. This view originates in the early Stoic thinker Chrysippus (279–206 BCE) who declared, "It is not true that there exists an art called medicine, concerned with the diseased body, but no corresponding art concerned with the diseased soul. Nor is it true that the latter is inferior to the former, in its theoretical grasp and therapeutic treatment of individual cases."[5]

So the Stoic *apatheia* is not a non-emotional state, but the state of the soul in which there are only ordered emotions. This is an essential Stoic insight into the nature of human emotion, one that is contrary to the philosophical tradition of Plato.

In Plato's view, all emotions were believed to be located in the irrational part of the soul, and thus must be controlled, and even suppressed, by the rational part of the soul, with the help of the spirited part.[6] In contrast, Stoic thinkers like Chrysippus and

4. Nussbaum, *The Therapy of Desire*, 13.

5. Ibid., 13–14. The original text is taken from Galen's *De Placitis Hippocratis et Platonis [PHP]* (*On the View of Hippocrates and Plato*), edited by P. De Lacy (Corp Medicorum Graecorum, vol. 4, 1–2; Berlin 1978–80).

6. Julie Annas analyzes Plato's theory of the human soul in her book, *An Introduction to Plato's Republic*. Plato divided the human soul into three parts: (1) the rational part is located in the head; this is the part that can reason and make judgment independently from the bodily senses and emotions; (2) the irascible part is located in the chest; this is the part that has courage to

Seneca did not believe that emotions were irrational; nor did they share the view with Plato that the human soul was divided into three parts, with three distinct faculties. Stoic scholar J. M. Rist observes that in contrast to Plato, Chrysippus held that every human choice and act involves both reason and emotion. There is no such thing as a purely rational act without emotion, nor an emotional response without an assent of the intellect.[7] If an emotion has become irrational, it could not be controlled by a rational faculty, as Plato held, for what is meant by "irrational" is precisely a state contrary to rationality. Indeed, this was the Stoics' conviction. For them, emotions were mental judgments and attitudes toward external things, and thus, to change them, one must change one's mental judgments and attitudes to the external things that have given rise to them. Such a change of judgment would require an education that leads to a change in personal traits, as well as a need for a self-discipline in practicing reservation of desires.[8]

Stoics identify four main passions: *distress, pleasure, fear,* and *appetite. Distress* is the judgment that there is something negative at hand and thus it is appropriate to feel a kind of contraction. In this sense, distress is a contrary movement to *pleasure,* which is a feeling that something positive is at hand and thus it is appropriate to feel an expansion. *Fear* is a judgment that something bad is at hand and thus it is appropriate to avoid it; whereas, *appetite* is the judgment that something good is at hand and thus it is appropriate to reach for it.[9] These four principal passions are further divided into sub-passions. *Distress* is expressed in such subsumed emotions as anger, bitterness, sexual disorder, and excessive love for power, wealth, and reputation. *Pleasure* can be expressed as a mean-spirited satisfaction and contentment in others' misfortunes.

carry out into action that which has been informed by the rational part; (3) the sensible part is located in the belly; this is the part that's often responding to the desire of the senses and thus ought to be controlled by the rational part of the soul with the help of the irascible part. See Annas, *An Introduction to Plato's,* 125–30.

7. Rist, *Stoic Philosophy,* 35.

8. Sorabji, *Emotion and Peace of Mind,* 54.

9. Ibid., 30.

Fear is experienced as a lack of courage and confidence and often presented by hesitation, agony, shame, panic, and fright. Finally, *appetite* comes as a result of unsatisfied desires and often manifests itself in envy, resentment, distress, sorrow, and anguish.[10] What is crucial to Stoics is that these four principal passions and their various manifestations are unnatural movements of the soul caused by ignorance and lack of self-discipline, and thus ought to be transformed into healthy emotions that are natural to the soul.[11]

The Stoic method for transforming these passions into healthy emotions, as discussed, presupposes an educational process that results in a correct understanding and attitude toward external reality. There is also a technique of applying the opposing forces as a way to counteract the movement of the soul under the influence of the passions. The technique presents the three main healthy emotions: *joy, caution,* and *wish* as the opposing forces to the passions. *Joy* is the opposite of *distress* and *pleasure*; it consists of being in a reasonable state in relation to *pleasure* and *distress.* *Caution* is the opposite state to *fear*; it is a state of being in reasonable avoidance of hardship, challenge, and shame. Finally, *wish* is the opposite state to *desire*; it is a state of striving in a reasonable way. The key word that describes these three healthy states of mind is *reasonable.* As noted, Stoics view passions as excessive emotions that have gone beyond the reasonable judgment of the mind. Their technique of counteracting the passions by their opposing forces is an effective way to "check" and "balance" the various emotions so that the healthy emotions can have the upper hand over the disordered emotions and be in the person's consciousness. The hope is that when *joy, caution,* and *wish* are all present in the person's consciousness, not only will they become the opposing forces to the passions, but they will guide and direct the person's choices and actions.[12] Seen from this perspective, the Stoic *apatheia* really is the state of spiritual joy and the most natural state of the human consciousness. The next chapter will study the transmission of

10. Inwood and Gerson, trans., *The Stoics Reader*, 138–39.

11. Ibid., 138–39.

12. Ibid., 120.

Stoic *apatheia* into the Christian tradition and how *apatheia* was interpreted in the spiritual theology of Evagrius Ponticus.

CHAPTER 2

Apatheia in Evagrius Ponticus

In this chapter we shall discuss the development of the Greek concept of *apatheia* in Evagrius Ponticus (345–399), a learned monk of the fourth century. But before doing so, it is important, first, to explore briefly how the concept of *apatheia* was interpreted for the spiritual theology of the early Christian theologians.

According to Richard Sorabji, it was Philo (20 BCE–50 CE), a Hellenistic Jewish philosopher, who first reflected on Stoic philosophy in his philosophical writings. Philo's writings became the primary Stoic-influenced source for the early church fathers' spiritual theology.[1] The general view of the fathers was that *apatheia* was the state of freedom of the soul from passions, a view very similar to that of the Stoics.

But there was a gradual shift in the early church tradition regarding the understanding of *apatheia*. According to Robert Wilken, Clement of Alexandria (150–215) understood *apatheia* as a state of complete eradication of all passions. This view originated in Clement's understanding that Jesus Christ himself was free of passions and thus his followers were encouraged to imitate him in this virtue.[2] This was a sidetrack from Stoic *apatheia*, for as dis-

1. Sorabji, *Emotion and Peace of Mind*, 343.

2. Robert L. Wilken, "Maximus the Confessor on the Affections in Historical Perspective," 412–13.

cussed, Stoics perceived *apatheia* not as a complete eradication of all emotions, but as the state of soul where healthy emotions, such as *joy, caution,* and *wish* exist. Further, Stoics conceived *apatheia* as the necessary condition for the attainment of a happy life. A Stoic sage was not a man without emotions; rather, his joy, caution, and wish constitute his sound emotional state. It was unfortunate that Clement had thought that *apatheia* was a complete eradication rather a transformation of passions. Either he did not understand the Stoics correctly, or he wanted to change the meaning of Stoic *apatheia* in order to adapt it to his Christian spiritual theology. If the latter, this is perhaps even more perplexing because neither Jesus nor the apostles either exemplified or advocated for such a passionless existence.

Subsequently, Origen of Alexandria (185–253) construed Seneca's "third movements"[3] not as "passions" but as "bad thoughts." He employed the Greek word *logismoi,* which is translated into English as "bad thoughts," to denote Seneca's third movements. Origen adapted the concept of *logismoi* from the Gospel of Matthew, where it says, "For out of the heart come evil intentions, murder, adultery, fornication, theft, false witness, slander" (Matt 15:19). The decisive shift from the Stoic concept of *pathe* (passion) to Origen's *logismos* (bad thought) was of crucial importance in that a bad thought was conceived not as a mere excessive emotion, as the Stoics would have, but as a temptation suggested by the devil that provoked an evil intention of the heart, and that, if not resisted, could lead to evil choices and actions.[4]

Evagrius Ponticus inherited this understanding of "passions" as "bad thoughts" from Origen of Alexandria and then further developed the concept of *apatheia.* Before exploring Evagrius's development of *apatheia,* it is important, first, to indicate briefly the context of his life and theological anthropology.

3. As discussed in Chapter 1, Seneca conceives the "third movements" as "excessive emotions" that have gone beyond the reasonable control of the mind. These movements are considered the "passions" by the Stoics.

4. Sorabji, *Emotion and Peace of Mind,* 147.

Evagrius was a disciple of the Cappadocian fathers, Basil the Great (320–379), Gregory of Nyssa (332–395), and Gregory of Nazianzus (329–389). He was ordained a reader by Basil, the bishop of Caesarea, and later was also ordained a deacon by Gregory of Nazianzus, the bishop of Constantinople.[5] There is no doubt that Evagrius was influenced by the theology of the Cappadocian fathers early on in his life. But perhaps he was more influenced by the theology of Origen, particularly by Origen's method for scriptural interpretation, than the doctrinal theology of the Cappadocian fathers.

Origen's method for scriptural interpretation identifies three levels of meaning in the biblical texts—the *literal*, the *ethical*, and the *spiritual* meanings. These three levels of meaning correspond to the three parts of the human soul in Plato's conception of the tripartite soul called *mind*, *spirit*, and *desire*. The mind is the reasoning part that loves wisdom; the spirited part is the center of courage and takes delight in victory and honor; and the desiring part loves sensible objects and is often blinded by its own desire for material things.[6]

Origen's method for scriptural interpretation has as its objective the deepening of the spiritual life of Christians. It was Evagrius who developed what were known as the three stages of spiritual practice—the *practical*, the *natural*, and the *theological* stages—to correspond to the Origen's three levels of meanings of spiritual text. Evagrius arranged these three stages of spiritual practice in a progressive order. The *practical* stage aims at the cultivation of virtues; the *natural* stage aims at the understanding the order of the created world; and the *theological* stage aims at the attainment of a total union with God. The three stages are mutually involved, but there is a hierarchy among them: the higher stages comprehend the lower ones.[7]

5. Sinkewicz, trans., *Evagrius of Ponticus*, xvii.

6. See Annas, *An Introduction to Plato's Republic*, 125–30.

7. Greer, trans., *Origen*, 23. I will explore Evagrius's three stages of spiritual practice in more detail later in this chapter.

Another influence of Origen on Evagrius was the idea of double creation: the first was called the creation of pre-existing souls and the second was the creation of the material world and human bodies. Origen believed that God created a certain number of souls before the creation of the world. Being negligent and forgetting of their nature as created in God's image, these pre-existing-souls eventually fell away from God into the created world which God had created. God, then, created a body for each of the fallen soul as both a punishment of the soul's fallen state and a means for the soul's spiritual journey back to God.[8] Evagrius adapted Origen's view of double creation in his development of spiritual theology. Consequently, there was also a dualistic tendency to perceive the human body as a mere means of the soul's spiritual journey back to God. For Evagrius, the ultimate aim of spiritual practice is the return of the soul to God in a complete detachment from the bodily senses and the material world.

Besides this important adaptation of Origen's view to his spiritual theology, Evagrius was also influenced by the ascetical tradition of the desert monks of the fourth century with whom he lived and practiced during the last fifteen years of his life in the desert of Egypt. It was during these years that Evagrius absorbed the ascetical practice of the desert monks, noticeably, Makarius of Egypt and Makarius of Alexandria.[9] These two monks embraced a severe form of ascetical practice from which Evagrius learned. Consequently, in Evagrius's spiritual theology, there is a blend of Origen's thoughts with the ascetical tradition of the desert monks.

The discussion of Evagrius's life and theological underpinning sets the context for the discussion on the development of his ascetical practice to which we now turn. At the heart Evagrius's spiritual practice one observes the development of eight bad thoughts or passions[10] and the method for countering them so as to attain *apatheia*. In his *On Discrimination in Respect of Passions*

---

8. Sinkewicz, *Evagrius of Ponticus*, xxxvii.

9. Ibid., xviii.

10. Evagrius uses "bad thoughts" and "passions" interchangeably.

and Thoughts (in short, *On Discrimination*),[11] Evagrius describes the eight thoughts and characterizes them as gluttony, fornication, avarice, envy, anger, *acedia*, vainglory, and pride. For Evagrius, these thoughts are the unnatural movements of the soul; they comprise the contrary state to that of *apatheia*. Further, Evagrius's central concern is the state of pure prayer, whereby the word "pure" implies the state of the soul uncontaminated by bad thoughts. For this reason, bad thoughts must be completely eradicated if prayer is to be productive.

Evagrius presents various methods for the eradication of bad thoughts. Most remarkable of all is his observation of the movements of these thoughts in the human soul. He is very perceptive and skillful in his observations here. The following text illustrates how crucial it is for a contemplative (one who prays) to be aware of the origin of bad thoughts and their movements so as to be ready to fight against them when they approach.

> Sit down and recall in solitude the things that have happened: where you started and where you went; in what place you were seized by the spirit of unchastity, dejection, or anger and how it all happened. Examine these things closely and commit them to memory, so that you will then be ready to expose the demon when he next approaches you. Try to become conscious of the weak spot in yourself which he hid from you, and you will not follow him again. (*On Discrimination*, 8)[12]

According to Evagrius, bad thoughts can be aroused by various ways. For example, an evil spirit can suggest bad thoughts by triggering the contemplative's memory, reminding him or her of an image from the past that often elicits one or more of the bad thoughts. For this reason, Evagrius advises that one should be vigilant and keeps watch of the movements of bad thoughts. For example, he writes, "When you pray, keep close watch on your

11. Evagrius Ponticus, "On Discrimination in Respect of Passions and Thoughts" in *The Philokalia*, vol. 1, trans. & ed., G.E.H. Palmer, Philip Sherrard and Kallistos Ware (New York: Faber and Faber, 1979), 38–52.

12. G.E.H. Palmer, *The Philokalia*, vol. 1, 43–44.

memory so that it does not distract you with recollections of your past. But make yourself aware that you are standing before God. For by nature the intellect is apt to be carried away by memories during prayer" (*On Prayer*, 45).[13] In another way, bad thoughts can also be caused by an object perceived through the external senses of touching, seeing, hearing, smelling, and tasting. In this regard, Evagrius observes, "All thoughts inspired by the demons produce within us conceptions of sensory objects; and in this way the intellect, with such conceptions imprinted on it, bears the forms of these objects within itself. So, by recognizing the object presented to it, the intellect knows which demon is approaching" (*On Discrimination*, 2).[14]

Besides being watchful of the origin and the movements of bad thoughts, a contemplative is advised to be patient, to do spiritual reading, and to pray the Psalms: "Psalmody calms the passions and curbs the uncontrolled impulses in the body; and prayer enables the intellect to activate its own energy" (*On Prayer*, 83).[15]

Finally, similar to the Stoics' method for counteraction, Evagrius believes that bad thoughts can be countered by good thoughts. For example, he writes, "Some thoughts are cut off, and sometimes they do the cutting off. Evil thoughts cut off good thoughts, and in turn are cut off by good thoughts" (*On Discrimination*, 6).[16] Evagrius often advises a monk who is prone to anger toward another monk to pray for him, because the prayer directed toward someone will often generate a good wish toward that person, which in turn brings about good intention in the person who prays for him. The good intention toward another person will eventually replace one's anger toward that person with charitable thoughts.

13. Evagrius Ponticus, *On Prayer* in Palmer et al., *The Philokalia*, vol. 1, 61. (Note: *On Prayer* is a compilation of 153 short sayings. The number 153 is believed to correspond to the disciples' catch of 153 fish at the command of Jesus, as is recorded in John 21:1–14. All citations from Evagrius's *On Prayer* will be taken from Palmer et al., *The Philokalia*, vol. 1.)

14. Ibid., 18–19.

15. Ibid., 65.

16. Ibid., 42.

These various ways of countering bad thoughts are effective methods that can assist the person in prayer. In other word, for Evagrius, the eradication of bad thoughts is not for its own sake, but for the attainment of *apatheia*, which is the state of prayer, as it is written, "The state of prayer is one of dispassion" (*On Prayer*, 53).[17] Dispassion is another word to describe the state of freedom from the passions, or *apatheia*. Seen from this perspective, prayer and discernment of bad thoughts are intricately related with the single aim: to attain the state of the human soul in union with God.

Further, taken from Origen's scriptural meanings and Plato's theory of soul in three parts, Evagrius conceives prayer as progressively developed in three stages: *practical, natural,* and *theological* stages. For example, he instructs, "Pray first for purification of the passions; secondly for deliverance from ignorance and forgetfulness; and thirdly, for deliverance from all temptation and dereliction" (*On Prayer*, 38).[18] There is a progression in terms of the degrees of spiritual growth in the three stages of prayer. The first stage aims at the purification of the disordered desires and to cultivate virtues; the second stage aims at the attainment of natural knowledge of created things; and the third stage aims at the soul's complete detachment from material things and total union with God. Evagrius describes the three stages as follows: "We practice the virtues [first stage] in order to achieve contemplation of the inner essences of created things [second stage], and from this we pass to contemplation of the *Logos* [the divine nature of Christ, third stage] who gives them their being; and He manifests Himself when we are in the state of prayer [*apatheia*]" (*On Prayer*, 52).[19] One observes that the three stages relate to one another in a progressive manner in which the higher stage comprehends the lower ones and the lower one functions as the necessary condition for the higher ones. The first stage of prayer results in *orderly love* of the created nature; the second results in *true knowledge* of the created nature; and the third results in complete *divine union* between

17. Ibid., 62.
18. Ibid., 60.
19. Ibid., 61–62.

the soul and God, which, in turn, enables the one who prays to comprehend the first two stages spontaneously.[20]

There is a further development in Evagrius's understanding of prayer. For him, the primary goal of spiritual practice is the detachment of the soul from the temptations of the body. This dualism between the soul and the body in Evagrius's spiritual theology is not new; he inherited this dualistic tendency from Plato's theory of reality whereby that which is true and real belongs to the "spiritual" realm, whereas, the realm of material, including the human body, is not real in that these are changeable, whereas what is real is unchangeable.[21] In this system of thought, the human mind (or *nous* in Greek) constitutes the essence of the human person, and the body is perceived as the means for the soul's manifestation of its intention and action. The intellect (*nous*) is conceived as the essence of the human person; its highest and most noble capacity is for "pure prayer," a stage of prayer without any lingering with the material world and the bodily senses. It is not surprising that Evagrius conceives the whole purpose of spiritual practice to be the purification of the intellect from the bodily senses so that the intellect may ascend to God. In fact, Evagrius insists that "prayer is the ascent of the intellect to God" (*On Prayer*, 36).[22] In his view, the intellect is not only capable but willing to return to God in a purely immaterial manner, independent of the bodily senses and material world (though this is not to be understood as a *literal* detachment of the soul from the body so much as an epistemic ascent beyond knowing through the senses). Any created thing, including the

20. Emphasis added.

21. The terms "real" and "not real" do not mean "existent" and "nonexistent" here. Rather, they signify the difference between things that are not changeable (for example, the idea of goodness) and changeable things (for example, particular good things, such as specific good people, good fruit, and good shoes). For Plato, the idea of goodness is fully real, whereas particular good things are not "real" in the sense that they are changeable and do not possess full reality. But they are not non-existent either. They are "in between" being and non-being.

22. Palmer et al., *The Philokalia*, vol. 1, 60.

conceptual images of them, can potentially impede the intellect in its return to God. This is the line of thought that leads Evagrius to state the following regarding prayer: "When you are praying, do not shape within yourself any image of the Deity, and do not let your intellect be stamped with the impress of any form; but approach the Immaterial in an immaterial manner, and then you will understand" (*On Prayer*, 67).[23]

To further understand and appropriate Evagrius's view on prayer, one needs to study his prayer method in the *Trilogy*. The *Trilogy* is a collection of three works on spiritual practice, built on each other in a progressive manner. In it, Evagrius gives instructions about the nature of prayer and its progress and goal.

According to Jeremy Driscoll, Evagrius's *Trilogy* is structured to reflect the gradual growth in the spiritual life of the monk in three stages. The *Praktikos* (or *practical* stage) is used for beginners in the spiritual life. Initially, the monk's spiritual practice aims at the cultivation of virtues and the establishing of the necessary foundation for the subsequent two stages. The method used in the *Praktikos* aims to help the monk to cleanse the passions in his soul: "The practical life is the spiritual method for purifying the passionate part of the soul" (*Praktikos*, 78).[24] The goal here is to set the soul free of the passions so as not to be dragged down by them. This is the first degree of *apatheia*; the passionless state in which the soul is free of the passions.

The *Gnostikos* (or *natural* stage), which is the second of the *Trilogy*, is a small transitional work between the *Praktikos* and the *Kephalaia Gnostica*, the third of the *Trilogy*. In this second work, Evagrius describes the second stage of spiritual practice, one that aims at the attainment of the knowledge of the natural world, as the word gnostic, or *gnosis*, which means "knowledge," suggests. Here, after being free of passions, the monk is able to contemplate God, not as immaterial, but as revealed in creation. Now the monk is able to discern the inner essence in the natural order of created things, which was hidden from him before because of the passions

23. Ibid., 63.
24. Sinkewicz, *Evagrius of Ponticus*, 110.

in his soul. The second stage signifies another degree of *apatheia*; it is not merely a state of freedom from the passions, as it was in the first stage, but a freedom from ignorance, which leads to an attainment of knowledge of created reality.[25]

The third and final stage in the spiritual growth of the monk (*theological* stage) is also called "pure prayer" in that it is the prayer of the mind in a completely immaterial manner. Its method is described in the *Kephalaia Gnostica* (the third of Evagrius's *Trilogy*) and Evagrius's other work, called *Skemmata*, (*The Sapphire Light of the Mind*).[26] According to William Harmless, Evagrius's "pure prayer" signifies the most radical view on *apatheia*, whereby *apatheia* is no longer viewed as a state of the soul free of the passions; nor is it conceived as a mere state of the mind free of ignorance of the created world, but as a state of the soul free of all emotions and imprints caused by the bodily senses. Here after being purified of all the passions and in the state of complete detachment from material reality, the soul is able to see its own light, independent of any material impressions.[27] Evagrius's method of "pure prayer" is here described as his own experience of a personal encounter with the pure light of the Holy Trinity: "Prayer is the state of the mind that comes to be from the single-light of the Holy Trinity" (*Skemmata*, 27).[28]

Two observations can be made in regard to Evagrius's prayer method. First, as already discussed, Evagrius defines the state of *apatheia* as the state of prayer, and prayer is structured according to the three progressive stages, with divine union as the final end. But divine union is perceived as a union of the contemplative's *mind* to the mind of God in an *immaterial* manner. One may pose the question, thus, what is the purpose of the human body and the material world if they were perceived as the mere means for the soul's spiritual practice in its journey to return to God? In other

25. Driscoll, *Steps to Spiritual Perfection*, 13.

26. Harmless, *Desert Christians*, 353.

27. Ibid., 354.

28. Harmless and Fitzgerald, trans., "The Sapphire Light of the Mind: The *Skemmata* of Evagrius Ponticus," 526.

words, Evagrius's prayer method in three stages seems to devalue the created world and the bodily senses.

Second, in Evagrius's three stages of prayer one observes a parallel between the three stages of prayer and the three degrees of *apatheia*. Just as prayer progressively develops in three stages, with the final stage conceived as a purely immaterial form, so too, *apatheia* is to be conceived in three degrees correspond to three progressive stages of prayer, whereby the final stage of prayer signifies a complete eradication of the bodily senses and emotions. This development, as we have seen, marks a departure from the Stoics' understanding of *apatheia* discussed in Chapter 1. There it was concluded that, for the Stoics, *apatheia* is not a non-emotional state of mind, but a state where the mind is free of disordered emotions and only good emotions remain. The Stoic sage is not a non-emotional person, but a person who is free of disordered emotions, while joy, caution, and wish, the three healthy emotions, remain and constitute the sound emotional state of his soul. The next chapter will present the spiritual theology of John Cassian, who in contrast to Evagrius, developed a prayer method and the understanding of *apatheia* as resulting from the heart rather than the mind.

CHAPTER 3

Apatheia in John Cassian

In the last two chapters we discussed the nature, function, and implementation of *apatheia* in the spiritual life, underscoring a common characteristic shared by both the Stoics and Evagrius Ponticus, namely, the perception of *apatheia* as a state of the mind free of disordered emotions. We also underlined the point that in the development of *apatheia* in Evagrius, there was a decisive step that diverged from the Stoic tradition in that for Evagrius *apatheia* signified a complete detachment of the mind from the bodily senses and the material world.

This chapter will examine the view of *apatheia* in the spiritual theology of John Cassian (360–435). Cassian was the theologian of the Eastern church who became influential in the transmission of the Greek monastic tradition to the Latin church in the West. The place of Cassian's birth is uncertain. Speculations among scholars seem to agree that he came from a Latin-speaking province in the East, which is now Romania.[1] In his early years, Cassian traveled with his older and close friend Germanus throughout North Africa, where they joined the community of monks in Egypt and learned spiritual practices from the learned monk Evagrius Ponticus (345–399), whose spiritual theology we studied in the last

---

1. Stewart, *Cassian the Monk*, 3–4. See also Feldmeier, *Christian Spirituality*, 109.

chapter.[2] Cassian was ordained a deacon in Constantinople, which is now Istanbul in Turkey. In his later years, Cassian travelled to Rome and Gaul and was ordained a priest. In 415 he founded two monasteries in Marseilles, a portal town in southern France, one for men and one for women. His two main works are the *Institutes* and the *Conferences*, both of which were written in Latin and addressed the monks in his monastic community. These works became the main source from which Saint Benedict, the founder of the Order of Benedict in the sixth century in Italy, composed the rules for his monastic community.[3]

Cassian inherited the spiritual theology of Origen of Alexandria from Evagrius Ponticus and was influenced by Evagrius's interpretation of Origen's thought. But there was a shift in Cassian's development that diverged from the Origenist system. Toward the end of the fourth century and the beginning of the fifth century, Evagrius's spiritual theology, especially his view on *apatheia*, had become controversial at least for two reasons. First, the Evagrian *apatheia* had been perceived by spiritual theologians as being too philosophical. Second, most theologians agreed that contemplation was a matter of the heart rather than the head; and they saw in Evagrius's spiritual practice a method of prayer that essentially developed as a mental exercise with the aim to free the mind from temptations of the body to the point of devaluing the bodily senses and the material world. This became an issue that had circulated among the theologians, and Cassian was aware of it.

Being a disciple of Evagrius for many years, Cassian learned from Evagrius's spiritual theology, but he reinterpreted Evagrius for his own spiritual theology. Cassian's distinctive development can be seen from his careful word choice. The Greek term *apatheia*, for him, was based on Evagrius's theological anthropology, one that undermined the intrinsic value of the created world and of human bodily senses. For this reason, Cassian avoided the word *apatheia* and instead employed the Latin term *puritas cordis*, which is translated into English as "purity of heart." Cassian's choice of *puritas*

2. Stewart, *Cassian the Monk*, 11.

3. Palmer et al., *The Philokalia*, vol. 1, 72.

cordis was inspired by Jesus's teaching in the Beatitudes: "Blessed are the pure in heart, for they shall see God" (Matt 5:8). The employment of this Latin term shows Cassian's tendency toward the West and his biblical approach to spirituality.[4]

Cassian's attempt to direct prayer away from the head toward the heart and his insistence on the need for God's grace in the pursuit of spiritual life can be perceived in contrast to Evagrius. Unlike Evagrius, who conceived the ultimate goal of spiritual practice as the return of the human mind to the mind of God in a purely immaterial manner, Cassian, by avoiding the term *apatheia* and using the term *puritas cordis*, has shifted the focus of spiritual practice away from being a purely *mental* prayer to a more *heartfelt* prayer, and underscores *love of God*, rather than *knowledge of God*, as the essential element in the union between God and the person who prays.[5]

Furthermore, unlike Evagrius, who could be understood to have implied that the ultimate goal of spiritual practice could be attained by mere human effort without the need for divine help, Cassian saw a great danger in focusing on the structures and practices to the extent that the person could lose sight of the truth that he or she must depend on God's grace.[6] This insight was clearly brought out in the *Eleventh Conference* in which Cassian addressed the monks in his community in regard to the vow of chastity. There he offered two specific directives. First, the monk should rely on God's grace to live a chaste life. His or her struggle to fight against the temptation of the flesh will not produce a pure heart; rather, it is God's grace that brings about the purity of heart in the monk. Second, Cassian distinguishes between love of God and others on the one hand, and fear of God's punishment on the other. The former ought to be the monk's motivation and grounding principle in living a chaste life; whereas he or she ought to avoid the latter (*Conf.* 11: 8).[7]

---

4. Stewart, *Cassian the Monk*, 42–43.

5. Ibid., 44 (Emphasis added).

6. Ibid., 19.

7. Luibheid, trans., *John Cassian: Conferences*, 146–47. Hereafter, citations

Unlike Evagrius, who conceived the ultimate goal of spiritual practice to be the union of the human mind to the mind of God, in his *First Conference*, Cassian distinguishes between the two kinds of goal in spiritual practice, based on Matthew 5:8.[8] There he says that the ultimate goal is the "vision of God," but the more immediate goal is the "purity of heart" (*Conf.* 1:4, 5–6).[9] He employed two Latin words, *destinatio* and *finis* to preserve the distinction between the two kinds of goal, whereby *distinatio* denotes the proximate goal while *finis* signifies the ultimate end.[10] The two goals are interdependent and condition each other. Purity of heart must be chosen as the target to which the monk should aim; as Cassian states, "We must follow completely anything that can bring us to this objective, to this purity of heart, and anything which pulls us away from it must be avoided as being dangerous and damaging" (*Conf.* 1:5, 3).[11] The vision of God, on the other hand, is perceived as the end of human life on which the final goal of spiritual practice should rest. But this final goal depends on the proximate goal, or the "purity of heart," and cannot be attained without it.[12]

The discussion on the different approaches between Cassian and Evagrius in regard to the ultimate goal of spiritual practice is crucial in understanding Cassian's view on *puritas cordis* (purity of heart). For Cassian, humility is the primary and guiding virtue in the attainment of *puritas cordis*. Cassian advises the monk in the monastic community to embrace humility in a form of obedience to his or her elder and more experienced monk. He underscores

taken from Cassian's *Conferences* will be cited as *Conf.* followed by the number of the particular *Conference*, the number of the section in that *Conference*, and a paragraph number.

8. Cassian composed twenty-four *Conferences*. In these conferences, Cassian presented the conversations between an older monk in the community and the young monks. Each conference often begins with a question raised by a younger monk and is followed by an answer in a form of a teaching by an older monk. (See Stewart, *Cassian the Monk*, 30).

9. Luibheid, trans., *John Cassian: Conferences*, 39.

10. Stewart, *Cassian the Monk*, 38.

11. Luibheid, trans., *John Cassian: Conferences*, 40.

12. Stewart, *Cassian the Monk*, 38.

the danger of deception when a monk decided to ignore the advice of an elder monk and to trust his own judgment. Cassian observes, "For the Devil drags a monk headlong to death by way of no other sin than that of submission to private judgment and neglect of the advice of our elders" (*Conference* 2:11, 10).[13] Lawrence Cunningham elaborates on this point, indicating that authentic spiritual discernment from the monastic tradition represented by Cassian derives from genuine humility. Cunningham underscores Cassian's insistence on the important role of elder monks in the community. For Cassian, spiritual discernment was never reduced to the individual's inspiration, but must stand in the tradition held by the community.[14] This communal-discernment aspect had humility as its guiding principle in the monk's spiritual practice with the aim of attaining the purity of heart.

In his *On the Eight Vices*, Cassian describes the vices (gluttony, lust, avarice, anger, envy, boredom, self-love, and pride), which he has taken from Evagrius's eight passions. Cassian also presents and explains the causal connection among the various vices and indicates a method for eradicating them.[15] The method employs the "technique of opposition," or in Latin *agere contra*, which means "to go against." According to this method, one should apply a corresponding virtue to fight against a particular vice. For example, gluttony, which manifests itself in excessive desire for food and drink, can be countered by the virtue of moderation. Cassian advises that those who are prone to take too much food and drink to restrain themselves from the intake of food and drink, and this can be done by fasting. However, one should strike a balance between the intake and restraint of food and drink by eating and drinking moderately. Neither of the extremes proves to be conducive to the fight against the vice of gluttony (*On the Eight Vices*).[16] Another

13. Luibheid, trans., *John Cassian: Conferences*, 72.

14. Cunningham, "Cassian's Hero and Discernment," 234–35.

15. John Cassian, *On the Eight Vices*, in Palmer et al., *The Philokalia*, vol. 1. Hereafter, citations from Cassian's *On the Eight Vices* will be taken from this text.

16. Palmer et al., *The Philokalia*, vol. 1, 73.

example of the use of *agere contra* can be seen in Cassian's suggestion on how to deal with the vice of self-love. But here the method applies a slightly different spin: instead of using humility to eradicate pride, Cassian advises that one can apply lust (excessive sexual desire) instead. In his view, lust and pride do not co-exist; one vice will cancel out the other, precisely because lust often leads one to realizes his or her weakness in the struggle against the sin of the flesh. When one realizes one's weakness, thought of pride will disappear and be replaced by the thought of humility before God.[17]

Similar to Evagrius, Cassian shares the view that the eight vices are unnatural movements of the soul. If not eradicated, these vices can lead a person to sinful acts. Consistent with the tradition of the early spiritual theologians, Cassian shares the view that the sinful acts themselves do not destroy the person's nature, which has been created by God as good. For example, in regard to the vice of lust, Cassian observes:

> Movement in the sexual organs was given to us by the Creator for procreation and the continuation of the species, not for unchastity; while incensive power was planted in us for our salvation, so that we could manifest it against sickness, but not so that we could act like wild beasts towards our fellow human beings. Even if we make bad use of these passions, nature itself is not therefore sinful, nor should we blame the Creator. A man who gives someone a knife for some necessary and useful purpose is not to blame if that person uses it to commit murder. (*On the Eight Vices*)[18]

The text just quoted addresses the vice of lust, but also indirectly explains the nature of the human will. God created the human will as good, but since God does not coerce the person to choose and act in one way or another, the person is disposed to choose and act according to his or her will. The will, however, can be misused, and when it is, evil comes as a consequence.

17. Stewart, *Cassian the Monk*, 66.
18. Palmer et al., *The Philokalia*, vol. 1, 72.

The question thus arises, what causes the will to choose evil rather than good? Clearly *God* cannot cause evil because God is good. Only evil can cause evil. In this regard, Cassian agrees with Evagrius that the cause of passions originates in the evil spirit. But in his analysis of the various causes of passions, Cassian also diverges from Evagrius. The most notable difference between the two theologians resides in their respective theological anthropology. As discussed in the last chapter, Evagrius conceives the mind to be the essential element that constitutes the human person. Divine union, for Evagrius, is perceived in terms of a *noetic* union in which the human mind is united to the mind of God in a purely immaterial manner. In contrast, Cassian directs prayer toward the heart, where, according to him, intentions can be provoked. Divine union, for Cassian, takes place in the heart. For this reason, the heart must be purified of its vices, for as noted earlier, *puritas cordis* (purity of heart) is the condition for the attainment of divine union.

Cassian observes, "In the first place, we must take the utmost care to guard the heart from base thoughts, for, according to the Lord, 'out of the heart proceed evil thoughts, murders, adulteries, unchastity, and so on'" (Matt 15:19). Cassian's observation stresses the importance of the intention of heart because it is within the heart that good or evil can be generated. In this regard, Cassian's teaching is more consistent with Jesus's teaching in the Gospel when the latter commands the crowds, saying, "Listen and understand: it is not what goes into the mouth that defiles a person, but it is what comes out of the mouth that defiles" (Matt 15:10). Jesus's teaching here underscores the importance of the intention of the heart where conscience can be informed and judgement can be made. This teaching does not imply that external reality has no impact on a person's consciousness. But it does help clarify the problem of good and evil by redirecting the problem to its proper place and by situating the problem in the intention of the will rather than an external reality. Cassian is very keen on this insight, and he advises that one needs to be aware of the movement of a bad thought from within one's heart and to cut off the thought as soon as one is aware of it. The longer a bad thought lingers, the more difficult it becomes to resist the thought. It is also often the case that the longer the thought lingers, the more likely one will be to assent to it, and once there is an assent, the mind will generate the various means by which an evil act can be carried out (*On the Eight Vices*).[19]

Of the eight vices, anger is the one Cassian discusses with greater length. The first advice Cassian offers is that one should not avoid a person toward whom one feels angry. It is only natural that one wants to avoid another toward whom one feels angry because the appearance of that person, either in reality or in imagination, can provoke the thought of anger in one's heart. But Cassian does not agree with this approach. Rather, he offers a contrary approach to the situation as can be seen in the following observation:

> When we are angry with others we should not seek solitude on the grounds that there, at least, no one will provoke us to anger, and that in solitude the virtue of long-suffering can easily be acquired. Our desire to leave our brethren is because of our pride, and because we do not wish to blame ourselves and ascribe to our own laxity the cause of our unruliness. So long as we assign the causes for our weaknesses to others, we cannot attain perfection in long-suffering. (*On the Eight Vices*)[20]

This advice is also applicable to the vice of envy, which is closely associated with anger. When dealing with these two vices, Cassian demonstrates his primary principle, namely, it is not so much the external reality (i.e., the person toward whom one is angry and envious) that causes the vice. Rather, it is the internal dynamism that gives rise to the ill intention in one's heart, which, in turn, causes the vice. In light of the principle, Cassian insists that in order to eradicate the vice, one must first purge the ill intention in the heart. Only then can the heart be healed of the sickness caused by anger and envy toward the other person. Avoiding the person toward whom one feels angry or envious will not heal one's

19. Palmer et al., *The Philokalia*, vol. 1, 76.
20. Ibid., 84.

heart from the sickness; it only hides the anger or envy from within and becomes escalated over time rather than diminished. Cassian writes, "When we try to escape the struggle for long-suffering by retreating into solitude, those unhealed passions we take there with us are merely hidden, not erased; for unless our passions are first purged, solitude and withdrawal from the world not only foster them but also keep them concealed, no longer allowing us to perceive what passion it is that enslaves us" (*On the Eight Vices*).[21]

Finally, Cassian agrees with Evagrius that anger and envy can impede prayer. The monk's goal in spiritual practice is to attain the state of union with God through prayer. Everything that can potentially impede his/her prayer ought to be eradicated. But here, too, there is a difference between Cassian and Evagrius in terms of their views on divine union. For Evagrius, as already discussed, divine union is perceived as a *noetic* union, whereby the mind of the contemplative is united to the mind of God in an immaterial manner. On the contrary, for Cassian, as noted, prayer arises from the good intention of the heart rather than from the understanding of the mind. The central concern for Cassian is the pure heart because only the heart that is pure can become the temple of the Holy Spirit (*On the Eight Vices*).[22] One can see why Cassian advises the contemplative not to have a thought of anger for whatever reason. Rather, one should not only uproot the thought of anger toward another human being, but also eradicate any anger toward even an inanimate object (*On the Eight Vices*).[23] This is the only way that the heart can be healed of the sickness caused by anger.

In the discussion on the vice of boredom, Cassian offers different advice from that discussed up to this point. There, instead of encouraging a person not to avoid someone toward whom he or she feels angry and envious, Cassian suggests that in the case of boredom, one should avoid seeking out others for advice. The reason is that boredom can effectively be healed through prayer, patience, and hard work, which one should and can do in solitude.

21. Ibid., 85.
22. Ibid., 86.
23. Ibid., 85.

To seek out others for advice in the case of boredom proves to be an unsuccessful strategy because in boredom one's mind often wanders aimlessly. To seek out others with whom one can spend time often ends up in useless talks. Gossip has been proven to be an unhealthy habit in the spiritual life. Thus, Cassian thinks that any advice offered by another person in the case of boredom can be proven to be ineffective. On the contrary, Cassian observes that boredom can be effectively countered with hard work, both physical and mental works, because the root of boredom is the wandering of the mind in useless distractions (*On the Eight Vices*).[24] Good labor can help refocus the mind and discipline the body in the case of boredom.

Of the eight vices, the vice of pride is the most cunning of all vices, according to Cassian. Unlike the first seven vices, which attack the person partially (each vice destroys a single virtue), pride attacks the *whole* person and destroys *all* virtues. When pride takes over the person, it is like the enemy in a battle who has taken over the entire city of the one who lost the battle. He infiltrates the whole city and takes control over every aspect of it. Cassian compares pride to a deadly plague that destroys not only part of the body but its entirety.[25]

The destructive characteristic of pride manifests itself in deceptiveness, particularly in people who think of themselves as advanced in the spiritual life. A well-trained and holy person can be deceived into thinking that he or she has attained perfection through prayer and spiritual practice. Cassian points out that this is the demon's tactic. It is the voice of the demon of pride speaking to the prideful person, provoking in him or her a sense of pride, and when pride has taken over, the foundation in spiritual practice is destroyed, for the person relies on his or her own effort and no longer relies on God's grace. In this case, humility proves to be the best weapon against pride. But in Cassian's analysis, it is not a mere kind of humility appropriated in recognizing one's weakness in

24. Ibid., 89.
25. Ibid., 92.

dealing with the vice of pride. Rather, it is more fundamental than that: a humility in realizing one's total dependence on God's grace in Jesus Christ to overturn pride. As Cassian observes, "When we have attained some degree of holiness we should always repeat to ourselves the words of the Apostle [Paul]: 'Yet not I, but the grace of God which was with me' (1 Cor. 15: 10)" (*On the Eight Vices*).[26]

In the final analysis, one sees that there is not a clear structure of prayer developed in three progressive stages as it was in Evagrius. Instead, in Cassian, *puritas cordis* (purity of heart) serves as the condition for prayer. This was the decisive move from Evagrius's *apatheia*, as discussed, and a prudent one that enabled Cassian to redirect prayer from the mind and refocus it on the heart. This refocus of the centrality of prayer serves as the foundation from which Cassian articulated his view on the eight vices and the various methods for countering and uprooting them. In doing so, Cassian was able to present a view on spiritual practice that underscored the human need for God's grace much more than that of Evagrius Ponticus.

The next chapter will study the spiritual theology of Maximus the Confessor, the seventh-century theologian whose theology marked a distinctive development, both in theory and practice, particularly in comparison to Evagrius.

26. Ibid., 93.

CHAPTER 4

Apatheia in Maximus the Confessor

Maximus the Confessor (580–662) was born of noble parents in Constantinople (present-day Istanbul in Turkey). He received a good education from an early age onward.[1] Polycarp Sherwood comments that the education Maximus received must have been a formal one, and would have consisted of the usual grammar, rhetoric, and philosophy, based chiefly on the works of Plato and Aristotle.[2] Sometime in his early 30s, Maximus became the first secretary to the Emperor Heraclius, the Byzantine Emperor, a position Maximus held for a few years, probably from 610 to around 614.[3] But Maximus's love for a life of solitude and his zeal for spiritual practice led to his departure from the Imperial Court.[4] In 614 Maximus joined a religious community in Constantinople and dedicated himself to the development of his own spiritual life and that of his fellow monks.[5]

In 626, the Persians invaded Constantinople. But Maximus, along with several fellow monks, had left Constantinople prior to

1. Louth, *Maximus the Confessor*, 4.

2. Sherwood, trans., *St. Maximus the Confessor*, 6.

3. Louth, *Maximus the Confessor*, 5.

4. Sherwood, trans., *St. Maximus the Confessor*, 7; Louth, *Maximus the Confessor*, 5.

5. Thunberg, *Microcosm and Mediator*, 3.

the invasion and arrived at Carthage, Africa, in 628.[6] In his later years Maximus was deeply involved in the *monothelite* controversies, which concerned the view that Jesus Christ has *one* nature and *one* will. Maximus disagreed with this view and argued for the *dyothelite* position, which supported the notion of *two* natures and *two* wills in Christ. Unfortunately, this involvement resulted in a series of trials, beginning in 655, and eventually led to Maximus's death in 662.

The reasons for Maximus's persecution were more political than religious. Disputes about the two wills of Christ had gone on for some time between the *monothelites* and the *dyothelites*. The former believed that Christ *could not* have two wills, a human and a divine, because they would conflict with one other. The latter, on the other hand, argued that Christ *must* have had two wills, since in Christ there were two natures, human and divine. The disputes between the two groups could not be easily resolved. The Emperor Constans II, who had succeeded the Byzantine Emperor, Heraclius, published a *Typos* in 647, which ordered that there should be no discussion or disputation regarding the theology of the wills of Christ.[7] Two years later Pope Martin of Rome convened the Lateran Synod, which condemned the *Typos*. Maximus lived in Rome at the time, and, along with Pope Martin, refused to accept the *Typos*. This resulted in the arrest of both Pope Martin and Maximus for non-compliance with the Emperor. Maximus was exiled to Lazika, an island on the Southeast coast of the Black Sea, and died on August 13, 662. Less than two decades after his death, the Council of Constantinople III (680–681) was held, and Maximus's doctrine of the two wills of Christ was vindicated and recognized as canonical.[8]

Maximus lived in a civilization that valued tradition, and he himself embodied this attitude. He inherited his method for the interpretation of Scripture from Origen, the ascetical tradition from Evagrius, the dogmatic tradition from the Cappadocian

6. Prassas, trans., *St. Maximus the Confessor's Questions and Doubts*, 6–7.

7. Ibid., 7.

8. Ibid., 7–8.

fathers, and the tradition of cosmic theology from Dionysius (or Denys) the Areopagite. Dionysius's identity and origin is unknown, though scholars agreed that he must have lived between the fifth and sixth centuries.[9] The theological synthesis of Maximus shows a process of seeking, articulating, and choosing from the various trends of theology in the Christian tradition that which he considered authentic and useful to the understanding of the Christian faith, while correcting that which he thought had been inconsistent with the faith. As a result, in Maximus's theological synthesis there is a restructuring of the Christian tradition in such a way that seemingly unrelated ideas and insights from the past become interconnected, as von Balthasar observes: "Thinkers of the class of Maximus Confessor are not simply trivial compilers or passive reservoirs; they are creators, who can work, surely, with traditional material but who also know how to arrange the pieces according to their own architectural design."[10]

To understand and appreciate Maximus's theological insights, it is appropriate, first, to consider the cultural and theological context in which he lived. As noted, Maximus lived during a time in the history of the church when there had already been many debates among the theologians on the nature and salvific work of Jesus Christ in the lives of Christians. Five different ecumenical councils of the church had already taken place: Nicaea I (325), Constantinople I (381), Ephesus (431), Chalcedon (451), and Constantinople II (553). These Councils articulated and defined the Christian faith based on the biblical tradition and the philosophical tradition employed by the church, with the aim to defend the faith against various heretical movements. Among these various councils, the Council of Chalcedon was probably the most important one for Maximus as it addressed the essential question concerning the overall theological foundation of his spiritual

9. The original Dionysius was an Athenian convert of St. Paul (Acts 17:34), whose identity this later, influential author assumed in his writings. Thus, scholars sometimes refer to him as Pseudo-Dionysius.

10. Balthasar, *Cosmic Liturgy*, 57.

theology, namely, how the two natures of Jesus Christ are united in the one divine person. The Council declared that the two natures of Jesus Christ are united in his divine person in an unconfused, unchangeable, undivided, and inseparable manner.[11] Maximus's spiritual theology was grounded on this foundational doctrine.

But as noted, Maximus also inherited the ascetical tradition from Evagrius, in particular, Evagrius's three stages of spiritual progress and the role of *apatheia* in this process. In his development, however, Maximus differed from Evagrius in one essential way. Unlike Evagrius, who perceives divine union in light of the union of the human mind with the mind of God, Maximus conceives divine union as a union of love. The principal purpose in Maximus's spiritual practice can be perceived as a progress in which self-love is transformed into altruistic love. Maximus conceives self-love as the mother of all passions; whoever is dominated by self-love is also under the influence of other passions (*Centuries on Love*, II:8).[12] Self-love often manifests itself in the forms of other passions, such as love for material things (avarice), excessive intake of food and drink (gluttony), excessive sexual pleasure (lust). Even anger and envy are manifestations of self-love in Maximus's view, because a person may be angry and envious toward another, but the motivation that gives rise to anger and envy comes from self-pity. Maximus is keenly aware of how destructive self-love can be. He constructs an ascetical practice with the aim to reverse the order of self-love to the state of altruistic love.

Following the ascetical tradition inherited from Evagrius, Maximus structures a method for contemplation in three progressive stages: the *practical*, the *natural*, and the *theological* stages. Maximus calls the first stage by two different names, either "self-mastery" or "ascetical struggle." The goal of the first stage is twofold: (1) to fight against the tendency of the *gnomic* will (a will under

11. Davis, *The First Seven Ecumenical Council (325–787)*, 187.

12. Palmer et al., *The Philokalia*, vol. 2, 66. See also Sherwood, trans. *St. Maximus the Confessor*, 83. Hereafter citations from Maximus's *Centuries on Love* will be taken from Palmer's translation, cited with a Roman number to indicate the number of the chapter, followed by the number of the paragraph in that chapter.

the influence of the passions) in its inclination toward self-love, and (2) to establish virtues. In other words, "ascetical struggle" helps restrain disordered desires (or passions) in the person and enables him or her to cultivate good desires that are necessary and useful for moral and spiritual development. The outcome of the first stage is the state of *apatheia*, the calm of ordered faculties now responding only to those things that are good and worthwhile.[13]

Similar to Evagrius and Cassian, Maximus identifies the eight passions as gluttony, lust, avarice, anger, envy, boredom, self-love, and pride. He also agrees with his predecessors that these passions are unnatural impulses of the mind toward created reality (*Centuries on Love*, I:35).[14] In his method, Maximus also employs the "technique of opposition," in Latin *agere contra*, as an effective method for eradicating the eight passions. However, as we shall see, Maximus's distinctive development, in comparison to Evagrius, can be discerned in his method for *transforming* the passions, rather than eradicating them altogether.

One observes in Maximus's theological anthropology the three distinct but interrelated faculties that constitute the human person: the intellect, the senses, and the desire of the will (*Centuries on Various Texts*, II:25).[15] He articulates the interrelation between the intellect and the will: since passions are the unnatural movements of the intellect toward created reality, the *gnomic* will is the will informed by an intellect that has been under the influence of the passions.

As already noted, for Maximus, the root of all passions is self-love, a love generated by the disordered desire of the *gnomic* will. In the first stage of spiritual practice, known as the *practical* stage, Maximus presents a remedy for the sickness of self-love by transforming self-love into altruistic love. The technique of opposition is applied by coordinating the interaction among the intellect, the senses, and the desire of the will. As a general principle, the higher

13. Sherwood, trans., *St. Maximus the Confessor*, 86.

14. Palmer et al., *The Philokalia*, vol. 2, 56.

15. Ibid., 193. Hereafter citations from Maximus's *Centuries on Various Texts* will be taken from the same translation.

faculty of the soul (the intellect) should direct the lower faculty (the senses), so that the will can choose according to its natural inclination. Maximus observes that every passion has a corresponding sensible object or a mental image of it. For example, without food or the memory of food there is no gluttony, and without gold or the memory of gold there is no disordered love for money that comes from the desire to exchange gold for money. This is true to any other corresponding sensible object and the passion implanted in the mind by means of the object. (*Centuries on Various Texts*, III:3).[16]

In his remedy of the passions, Maximus distinguishes between the sensible object and the passion arisen from it. In his analysis, the passion (or disordered desire) for created things does not originate in the thing itself, for every created thing is created by God as good. But evil can implant the disordered desire for a created thing in the mind by means of the corresponding sensible object or a mental image of it. So the root of the passion is neither in the human intellect nor in the object of the desire of the will, but in evil, which has implanted the passion in the intellect. In effect, the intellect is darkened and thus, unable to recognize the essence in created reality as it should. The danger of a passion, therefore, is that it can weaken the intellect from recognizing the essence of things, and the will, which is informed by the ignorance of the intellect, suffers as a result, and inevitably chooses that which is informed by the intellect, which in this case, is an act against the will's own nature.

Maximus's method for prayer begins with the recognition of the ignorance of the intellect as the result of the passions. His immediate advice is that one should not stop short at the level of appearance of created reality, but by means of contemplation (prayer) one should move the intellect toward seeing created things as images of spiritual realities:

> If instead of stopping short at the outward appearance
> which sensible things present to the senses, you seek with
> your intellect to contemplate their inner essences, seeing

16. Ibid., 210.

them as images of spiritual realities or as the inward principles of sensible objects, [then] you will be taught that nothing belonging to the visible world is unclean. For by nature all things were created good. (*Centuries on Various Texts*, I:92)[17]

The second stage of spiritual contemplation, known as the *natural* stage, should come as the natural outcome of the first stage. But Maximus makes a cautious remark about the connection between the first and second stages and insists that unless one has purified one's passions and achieved some degree of *apatheia*, one ought not move on to the second stage of prayer. He writes:

Until you have been completely purified from the passions, you should not engage in natural contemplation through the images of sensible things: for until then such images are able to mold your intellect so that it conforms to passion. An intellect which, fed by the senses, dwells in imagination on the visible aspects of sensible things becomes the creator of impure passions, for it is not able to advance through contemplation to those intelligible realities cognate with it. (*Centuries on Various Texts*, II: 75)[18]

Maximus knows from experience that often in the second stage of spiritual contemplation, one finds oneself returning repeatedly to the sensible objects or mental images of them for spiritual ratification. This condition, for Maximus, indicates that one's intellect has not yet been completely free of the disordered desires for the sensible objects of created things, and thus he advises that one should not move on to the second stage of contemplation, but should continue purifying one's passions from the sensible objects until one is completely free of the passions arising from them.

Once the intellect is free of its passions, then the *essence* of sensible objects will be revealed to the intellect, and once the intellect possesses its true knowledge of the sensible objects, then the will is informed with their goodness and thus is able to choose

17. Ibid., 185.
18. Ibid., 203.

them for what they truly are. This is the outcome of the second stage of spiritual practice, which cannot take place without the purification of the passions in the first stage. There is a gradual development in the person's capability to see created things for what they truly are in the second stage. The mind is now capable of perceiving the *logos* (or the essence) of created things, which it couldn't perceive before because of the influence of the passions. Maximus observes, "The intellect, once totally free from passions, proceeds undistracted to the contemplation of created beings, making its way towards knowledge of the Holy Trinity" (*Centuries on Love*, I: 86).[19]

In the third and final stage of spiritual contemplation, a different kind of knowledge is produced than that produced in the first two stages. In the first stage, one's knowledge is gained by means of the spiritual struggle against the passions that results in the cultivation of virtues. In the second stage, one knows created reality by means of the intellect which has been freed from the disordered desires of created things. But in the third stage, there is a revealed knowledge that goes beyond the grasp of intellect. This is a spiritual knowledge described as an "unknown knowledge" in that it is not gained by the intellect, but is infused by God's grace. Thus, one observes that the three stages of spiritual contemplation are related to each other in a gradual manner, in which the higher level *depends on* the lower levels and *completes* the lower levels. But the outcome of each stage is distinct from that of the other two stages, as can be seen from the following description:

> He who is not affected by changes in sensible things practices the virtues in a manner that is truly pure. He who does not permit the outward appearances of sensible things to imprint themselves on his intellect has received the true doctrine of created beings. He whose mind has outstripped the very being of created things has come, as a true theologian, close to the One [God] through unknowing. (*Centuries on Various* Texts, I: 93)[20]

19. Ibid., 63.
20. Ibid., 186.

The final stage is called *theological* contemplation in that it is no longer a work by mere human effort, but is the work of grace. Nonetheless, it presupposes the first two stages of spiritual practice in which human effort is required. The difference between the third stage and the first two can be seen in the shift in perspective. In the first two stages, one perceives created reality with God's grace; in the third stage one sees created reality as God sees.

Methodologically, Maximus makes use of Evagrius's three stages of spiritual progress, as discussed in Chapter 2 of the book. But, unlike Evagrius, Maximus insists on the unity of spiritual and material realities, and thus he avoids dualism. In Maximus's view, the spiritual reality provides the structure for spiritual practice, and spiritual practice in turns helps actualize the spiritual aspect of created reality. The state of *apatheia* is necessary for a life of love for God and others. But love is a desire of the heart, and desire can only be generated by the intention of the will. For this reason, unlike Evagrius, who perceived *apatheia* as the state of the mind free of the bodily senses and the created world, Maximus conceives desires as the constitutive elements of spiritual practice. *Apatheia*, in Maximus's terminology, is not so much a freedom of the mind from created reality, but *the freedom of the will from the passions*. *Apatheia* does not mean "lack of emotion," but a state of the soul where the passions are transformed into love.

Maximus is more concerned with the *transformation* of desires and the *right use* of desires than their eradication. *Apatheia*, for Maximus, is not the state of non-desire. On the contrary, the desires of the will remain, but their object changes from that of corporeal things *in and of themselves*, to God and the love of corporeal things *as created by God*.[21] One loves created things *as God's creatures*, reflecting God's own image and likeness. This kind of love is possible only if one has attained *apatheia* through contemplation.

Seen from this perspective, Maximus shares the Stoics' view on *apatheia*. As we saw in Chapter 1, the Stoic *apatheia* is not a non-emotional state; but it is the state of the mind free of excessive

21. Emphasis is mine.

emotions, while the three good emotions, *joy, wish,* and *caution* remain. Scholars specializing in Maximus's thought have observed that Maximus makes use of the Stoics' three good emotions of *joy, wish* and *caution* in his articulation of human emotions.[22] Like the Stoics, Maximus preserves these emotions, but he distinguishes them by their two different movements: one toward the good and the other away from the evil. *Joy, wish,* and *caution* are good and genuine human emotions. In Maximus's view, these emotions are the constitutive elements of the soul in tranquility and they can be used to counter the passions of the soul for the purpose of reorienting and redirecting the passions to the love of God and others.[23]

The distinctive development in Maximus, as compared to the Stoics and Evagrius, can be seen from his view on *deification,* or *divinization* (human transformation into divine likeness). This is a theological concept rooted in God's purpose for humanity, that God created human beings and became human in Jesus, so that in and through Jesus, human beings may become like God though the process of *deification.* The goal of human life is to become like God by means of the union with God in Jesus Christ. This union presupposes God's grace as its ultimate condition, but human effort in spiritual practice is also necessary, especially in the attempt to achieve the state of *apatheia.*

In Maximus's process of deification, there is a teleological level in the development of the human being into the likeness of God. In light of this understanding, *apatheia* neither functions merely as the medication for the soul's sickness, with the purpose to attain a life of knowledge and virtue, as in the view held by the Stoics; nor does it imply a devaluation of human bodily senses and the material world, as did in Evagrius's view. On the contrary, in Maximus's final stage of spiritual practice, human passions are retained and transformed into *agape,* or self-less love. This transformation of

22. Wilken, "Maximus the Confessor on the Affections in Historical Perspective," 416.

23. Blowers, "Gentiles of the Soul: Maximus the Confessor on the Substructure and Transformation of the Human Passions," 68.

the passions signifies a whole new level of spiritual development: the teleological level, as Blowers observes:

> Maximus deals with the passions from three intercon-
> nected perspectives—I shall call them physiological,
> existential (or moral-ascetic), and teleological—though
> not all three are always immediately in view in his indi-
> vidual expositions. For him, as for Gregory of Nyssa, it is
> plainly insufficient to ask where the passions originate,
> or what their physical or metaphysical status is, without
> considering at once their present modality and moral use
> (*praxis*) as well as their eschatological goal coincidental
> with the natural motion or appetitive drive of the soul
> toward God.[24]

There is an eschatological dimension in Maximus's final stage of prayer whereby human passions themselves are deified. *Deifica-tion* is a mode of spiritual union between God and a human be-ing in which human passions are not completely eradicated but retained and transformed into divine likeness. This view differs fundamentally from Evagrius's in that the Evagrius's *noetic* union signifies the condition in which the human mind is united to the mind of God in a purely immaterial manner, apart from the bodily senses and the material world. Maximus's development of *apatheia* also differs from the Stoic view on *apatheia* in that the *apatheia* in Maximus does not stop at the moral level, but continues progress-ing into the divine likeness and manifests itself in self-less love for others.

Lars Thunberg observes that Maximus has made the human passions the constitutive elements in the state of deification, and has placed them in the *heart*, rather than the mind, as Evagrius did. Both Evagrius and Maximus employed Plato's tripartite soul in the development of their respective prayer method. But they di-verged in their views on Plato. Evagrius's position reflected Plato's tripartite soul whereby the soul is divided into three parts: the rational, the irascible, and the sensible, but he coupled this with a Neoplatonic striving for the return of the human mind to the mind

24. Ibid., 66.

of God. This combination resulted in a separation between the rational part of the soul from both the irascible and sensible parts. Consequently, in Evagrius's view, *only the rational part* can be united with God, and in a purely immaterial manner. In contrast, Maximus conceived Plato's irascible part (the heart) as the center from which the desires of the will originate. In his view, both negative *and positive* emotions originate in the irascible part of the soul. For example, both anger (negative emotion) and courage (positive emotion) originate in the irascible part of the soul, but it is the characteristic of the irascible part to subordinate to reason, which is the function of the rational part of the soul.[25] For this reason, Maximus locates the primary source of the union between God and human being in the heart, or the irascible part of the soul, the center of human desires. Seen from this perspective, deification is not primarily the state of union of the human mind to the mind of God, but a stage in which human desires are restored and transformed into love.

This is the more why, as noted, the Council of Chalcedon in 451 became crucial for Maximus. The Council declares that the two natures of Christ are united in his divine person in an unconfused, unchangeable, indivisible, and inseparable manner. This statement means that the union of Christ's humanity and divinity is a *union-in-distinction* in which his two natures remain intact. The union enables the mode of communication between the two natures of Christ possible through what is known as *communicatio idiomatum*: What Christ does in his human nature, he does with the divine intention of the will, and what he desires with the divine will, he carries out in his human nature, without the two natures being confused with each other.[26] The *hypostatic union* is possible in Christ because of two reciprocal movements: the downward movement in the self-emptying of the divine reality in the Incar-

---

25. Thunberg, *Microcosm and Mediator*, 178–79. Here Maximus may be following Plato's view in the *Republic*, rather than Evagrius. For Plato, the soldier class are the social equivalent of this part of the soul, making courage one of their defining characteristics. And this is good so long as they submit to the philosopher kings (as this part of the soul submits to the rational part).

26. Davis, *The First Seven Ecumenical Council (325–787)*, 175–76.

nate Word, and the upward movement of the human reality of the Incarnate Word emptying itself into the divine reality. Both movements meet and unite in the one and same divine person of Christ. *Kenosis* (self-emptying) is required in both movements; but it is the divine initiative that enables the human to respond. Christ's human freedom is required because without it there is no free human response to the divine will. But because Christ's human freedom is united with his divine will unreservedly, Christ only chooses according to the intention of his divine will.

Maximus, then, draws an analogy between the *hypostatic union* of Christ's two natures and the union of an individual human person's will to the will of God in Christ. Maximus says that because of the hypostatic union of Christ's two natures the union between God and humans becomes possible in and through the grace of Christ. But Maximus distinguishes between the two modes of union. In the case of the union between God and humans, it is the union of two *natures;* whereas in the case of the union of Christ and God, it is the union of two *persons* of the Trinity. He employs the two terms, *ousiai* (natures) and *hypostases* (persons) to underscore the difference. First, the term *ousiai* (natures) signifies the two natures (human and divine) as a condition for the union between God and humanity; that is, union implies distinction as a condition. Without the existence of the two different natures there wouldn't be a need for union. Second, however, the union of the two natures (divine and human) is possible because of the *hypostasis* (the *Logos*) of the Second Person of the Trinity. This means that the incarnation of the *Logos* in the flesh of Jesus creates the possibility for the union of Jesus's two natures, first, and then by means of his grace, each individual person is capable of union with God through him.[27]

Thus, in Maximus's theology of deification, the teleological and eschatological state of spiritual union entails an ontological change in the human, whereby human passions are restored and transformed into the desire for God and the doing God's will, without thereby losing any of their human characteristics.

27. Cattoi, "An Evagrian *Hypostasis*?" 138.

Herein lies the essential difference between Evagrius and Maximus on the state of *apatheia*. Evagrius, in following what many take to be Origen's view, conceives the *eschaton* (the final purpose of God's plan for humanity) as the state of the human soul's cessation of movement and completely absorbed into the divine reality. In this state, human passions are not only eradicated but destroyed. The individual human identity is subsumed into the divine reality. In contrast, Maximus conceives the *eschaton* as the state of the soul's "ever-moving repose" around God. In this state, the only desire of the soul is the desire for God, which is also the soul's desire in the most natural state as God has created it.

This chapter explored Maximus's understanding of *apatheia* in his overall spiritual theology. Maximus's view was compared and contrasted with that of his predecessor, Evagrius. The central presentation aimed to articulate the difference between the two theologians in regard to their understandings of the state of divine union on which were grounded their respective views on *apatheia*. As demonstrated, Maximus located the center of divine union in the *heart* where human desires originated. This was contrasted to Evagrius's view on divine union in which the human *mind* was united to the mind of God. The difference between the two views necessarily led to two distinctive perceptions on the state of *apatheia*. Maximus's state of *apatheia* did not signify a complete eradication of human passions; rather, the passions were retained, transformed, and redirected to the love of God and others as created in God's own image and likeness. Evagrius's state of *apatheia*, in contrast, implied a complete eradication and destruction of the passions so that the mind alone could be united to the mind of God. Viewed from this foundation, prayer and spiritual discernment in both theologians, though are similar in many respects, were built on essentially different theological anthropologies.

The next chapter will explore the Ignatian concept of *indifferentia* (or "indifference" in English) and compare and contrast it to the concept of *apatheia* discussed thus far in the book.

CHAPTER 5

Apatheia in Ignatius of Loyola

Ignatius of Loyola (1491–1556), the founder of the Society of Jesus, whose members are known as the Jesuits, was born in Azpeitia in the Basque province of Guipúzcoa in northern Spain. His original name was Iñigo López de Loyola, the name he received when he was baptized, which is still kept in the parish church of Azpeitia.[1] Ignatius belonged to a noble family of Loyola.[2] According to Cándido de Dalmases, Ignatius was sent by his father, Beltrán Ibáñez de Oñaz, to Arévalo, a small town in the heart of Castile, at an early age to pursue an education he thought appropriate for the young Ignatius. It was here that Ignatius learned how to be a knight and an officer at a royal court. During the years of study, Ignatius must have read the books found in the library in Arévalo. This was a collection of religious books, romances, and tales of knightly deeds. These books had an impact on Ignatius's early life and helped form the young man into a courtly knight and a gentleman. Ignatius's early education, however, was more in keeping with the spirit of the world than of God, and had nourished in him a desire for vainglory and worldly fame.[3] The trajectory of his early

1. De Dalmases, *Ignatius of Loyola, Founder of the Jesuits*, 3.

2. Loyola was the name of the manor-house and farmland of Ignatius's ancestors (ibid., 4).

3. Ibid., 30–32.

life explained why, in his *Autobiography*, Ignatius saw vainglory as one of the dominant vices in his life against which he constantly struggled in order to seek the will of God.[4]

The turning point in the life of Ignatius took place during the battle against the French, who had claimed Pamplona, the territory in northern Spain, as their own. Ignatius was a captain leading Spanish troops fighting the French at the front line. In an attack by the French army, a cannonball hit Ignatius's right leg, causing a severe injury. The event happened on May 21, 1521, after which it took him six months to recuperate in his family castle at Loyola. During this period of recovery, Ignatius underwent a profound conversion, from a desire for great worldly achievements to a deep desire to serve God.

Ignatius was given two books to read as he was recovering. These were the *Vita Christi* (*The Life of Christ*) by Ludolph of Saxony, a fourteenth-century Carthusian, and the *Flos Sanctorum* (*The Lives of the Saints*) by Jacobus de Voragine, a thirteenth-century Dominican. The *Lives of the Saints* stirred a desire in Ignatius to do great things for Christ, as Saint Dominic and Saint Francis had done, while the *Life of Christ* supplied him with food for imaginative meditation, which required not merely mental pictures of the events in the life of Christ, but a level of "concentration and meditation capable of bringing to life the humanly comprehensible incidents in the life of Christ."[5]

One notices two different tendencies in Ignatius at this time in his life. First, his desires began to waver between worldly ambitions and doing great deeds for the glory of God. Second, Ignatius began to notice two different spiritual movements within his soul corresponding to the two competing objects of his desire, as they are recorded in his *Autobiography*:

4. There are several English translations of Ignatius's *Autobiography*. I use Parmananda R. Divarkar's translation entitled *The Pilgrim's Testament: The Memoirs of St. Ignatius of Loyola*. Hereafter, references from Ignatius's *Autobiography* will be taken from this translation, cited with *Auto* followed by a number of the paragraph.

5. Shore, "The *Vita Christi* of Ludolph of Saxony and Its Influence on the *Spiritual Exercises* of Ignatius of Loyola," 9.

> When he was thinking about those things of the world, he took much delight in them, but afterwards, when he was tired and put them aside, he found himself dry and dissatisfied. But when he thought of going to Jerusalem barefoot, and of eating nothing but plain vegetables and of practicing all the other rigors that he saw in the saints, not only was he consoled when he had these thoughts but even after putting them aside he remained satisfied and joyful. (*Auto* 8)[6]

This experience happened to Ignatius almost anytime he stopped reading and started reflecting on what he had read. He gradually became aware of two different spirits at work in him, attributing the cause of the feeling of dryness and discontentment to the evil spirit and the feeling of being consoled and content to God (*Auto* 8). He came to realize that the things in which he took delight had no lasting value, while the response to Christ instilled in him a desire to know the Lord better (*General Congregation* 35, Decree 2:4).[7] One observes that Ignatius became a new man whose passions for life remained the same, but the object of his passions changed (or was at least kept in tension) from worldly ambitions to the greater glory of God.

Inspired by the conversion at Loyola, Ignatius departed for Montserrat, where one night in March of 1522, on the feast of the Assumption of Mary, he decided to strip off his garments and give them to a beggar in exchange for the beggar's clothes. That night he knelt for hours in prayer before the altar of Our Lady (*Auto* 18). The next morning, Ignatius journeyed toward Manresa, a town in the province of Catalonia, located somewhere between Montserrat and Barcelona.[8] It was here in Manresa that Ignatius learned much about spiritual things. He recounted that it was here that God was teaching him like a school teacher teaches a child regarding spiritual matters (*Auto* 27). The origin of the *Spiritual Exercises* came

6. In his *Autobiography*, Ignatius writes in the third person and refers to himself as "he" and "him" rather than in the first person pronoun as "I" and "me." Thus, in the above cited text, the pronoun "he" refers to Ignatius himself.

7. Padberg, ed., *Jesuit Life & Mission Today*, 734.

8. Divarkar, *The Pilgrim's Testament*, 49n19.

from the experiences Ignatius had pertaining to God which he had written down in a notebook during the eleven months of his stay in Manresa.

Ignatius lived in sixteenth-century Europe, with its cultural shift from the late medieval period to the humanism of the Renaissance. Thus, he was a man of two ages, attempting to synthesize the insights he had acquired from both traditions.

As noted, during his recuperation Ignatius read the *Vita Christi* (*The Life of Christ*) of Ludolph of Saxony and was influenced by the Christological orientation of the book, in particular, its strong emphasis on the incarnation of God in Christ and what that might entail for the salvation of humanity.[9] It is not surprising that in the prelude to one spiritual exercise in the *Spiritual Exercises* Ignatius advised the retreatant to ask God for the grace to know what he or she wants, and in the contemplations on the incarnation of God in Jesus, Ignatius directed the retreatant to imagine the Gospel scene under consideration and to observe how Jesus interacted with the people. This opens to retreatant to being inspired by Jesus's words and deeds. Finally, Ignatius encouraged the retreatant to ask for the grace that he or she may come to *know*, to *love*, and to *follow* Jesus in his or her life.[10]

Scholars have also speculated that Ignatius might have been influenced by the *Devotio Moderna* (New Devotion) movement, in particular by *the Imitation of Christ* by Thomas à Kempis (1380–1471). *The Imitation of Christ* was a reaction against speculative

9. According to Charles Abbott Conway, Ludolph's doctrine of the incarnation emphasizes the centrality of the incarnation of God in the person of Jesus Christ, which entails the goodness of creation, in particular, the human bodily senses. In Ludolph's view, just as the bodily senses could be an occasion to sin, so too, they can be an occasion for a healing remedy. Other important aspects of Ludolph's theology of the incarnation include: the self-emptying of Christ in the mode of humility, and the inseparableness of the suffering of Christ and his glory. (See Conway, *The Vita Christi of Ludolph of Saxony and Late Medieval Devotion Centered on the Incarnation*, 8).

10. Emphasis added. The term "retreatant" refers to a person who undertakes the *Spiritual Exercises* of Saint Ignatius of Loyola in the context of a retreat. The retreat can last for as long as thirty days; but the most common form is structured for an eight-day retreat.

spirituality of the medieval period and an attempt to replace it with a strong affective piety.[11] We see this influence on Ignatius in the second annotation in the *Spiritual Exercises* when Ignatius states, "For what fills and satisfies the soul consists, not in knowing much, but in our understanding the realities profoundly and in savoring them interiorly" (*SpEx* 2).[12]

The third theological source that influenced Ignatius was the Christian Renaissance movement of the sixteenth century. Though Ignatius was a man rooted in the tradition of the late medieval period, he was also a man in touch with cultural movements of his own time and place, especially Renaissance humanism. In this regard, Ignatius might have been influenced by the trend of a new way of doing theology, known as *ad fontes* (return to the sources), advanced by the Christian humanists, notably Erasmus of Rotterdam (1469–1536). This trend of theology sought to retrieve, in reaction to the scholastic theology of Thomas Aquinas, the theological method of the early church fathers, which was more experiential, pastoral, and spiritual. This influence shows Ignatius's balanced synthesis between the speculative theology of Thomas Aquinas, which he and his first companions received during their years of formal philosophical and theological training at the University of Paris from 1528–35, and the new trend of theology expounded by the Christian humanists. Perhaps this is the reason Ignatius insisted that the theology suited for the formation of young Jesuits ought to show a synthesis of both traditions, for one can benefit from the clarity of understanding of the speculative theology of the scholastic tradition, while being moved to love

---

11. Healey, "The Imitation of Christ Revisited," 127.

12. Ignatius composed the *Spiritual Exercises* over a long period. These exercises reflected the spiritual movements Ignatius experienced and wrote down in his spiritual notes. There are several English and Spanish translations of the *Spiritual Exercises* of Ignatius of Loyola. I use George E. Ganss's translation, *The Spiritual Exercises of Saint Ignatius*. Hereafter, references from the *Spiritual Exercises* of Saint Ignatius will be taken from Ganss's translation, indicated with *SpEx* followed by a paragraph number.

and action by the theology of the early church fathers (*SpEx* 363; *Const.* 464).[13]

Finally, one needs to take into account the fact that before he took religious vows in 1534 and was ordained a priest in 1537, Ignatius was a layman. His experiences of God in Manresa reflected in the *Spiritual Exercises* were the experiences of a lay person. In them Ignatius described his own experiences of God with the aim to assist others who, like him, sought authentic meaning in their lives through a relationship with God. Seen from this perspective, the *Spiritual Exercises* were meant to be given to Christians, lay and religious alike, who desired to discern God's will for their lives in their own particular contexts.

The discussion on Ignatius's life, his conversion, and theological background provides the context for a consideration of his understanding of *apatheia*, to which we now turn. But before progressing further, the question arises: did Ignatius employ the term *apatheia* in his spiritual theology? Two considerations are relevant here. First, being a Spanish theologian who lived in the sixteenth century and who did not study Greek, Ignatius probably didn't feel the need to use the Greek term *apatheia* in the articulation of his spiritual practice, and indeed he didn't make use of the term. Second, however, Ignatius did employ the Spanish term *indifferentia* ("indifference" in English) three times in the *Spiritual Exercises*, the first time in the Principle and Foundation (*SpEx* 23:5); the second time in the Three Classes of Human Beings (*SpEx* 157:1); and the third time in the Election (*SpEx* 170:2). In all three instances, "indifference" is presented in relation to a choice one ought to make in the following of Christ: Ignatius insisted that in order to better choose Christ in the world and to serve God in Christ one ought to maintain the attitude of "indifference" to created reality. Ignatius described "indifference" as a necessary condition of the soul, detached from the disordered love for created things so that

---

13. Padberg, ed., *The Constitutions of the Society of Jesus and Their Complementary Norms*. Hereafter, references from *The Constitution of the Society of Jesus and Their Complementary Norms* will be taken from Padberg's edition, indicated with *Const.* followed by a paragraph number.

one may choose these things rightly. Further, the criteria for discerning the right use of these created things require the person to strive for a sense of spiritual disposition toward them. Seen from this perspective, the Ignatian *indifferentia* signifies a condition of the soul in tranquility, free from the disordered affections for created things, a similar condition of the soul in the state of *apatheia* discussed in the previous chapters.

The Ignatian understanding and use of the term *indifferentia* in the *Spiritual Exercises* might have been rooted in the Stoic philosophical tradition, retrieved by Erasmus in his *Enchiridion*, known as "The Manual of a Christian Knight." It was commonly accepted that Ignatius must have read the *Enchiridion* of Erasmus, during his time of study at Barcelona (1524–25) and Alcalá (1526–27). This was the common understanding among the early Jesuits, in particular, that of Goncalvez da Câmara, who states that Ignatius read and fully understood the *Enchiridion* at Alcalá, and did so with great care.[14] Renaissance historian John Olin observes that da Câmara's view is credible for two reasons. First, Erasmus composed the *Enchiridion* in Latin in 1501, and by the time Ignatius studied at Alcalá in 1526, Erasmus's book had been translated into Spanish. Thus, Ignatius would have read and understood the *Enchiridion* because it had been translated into his vernacular language. Second, Ignatius repeated his study of Latin at the College of Montaigu for reading comprehension when he first arrived at the University of Paris in 1528. Thus, he would have read the *Enchiridion* not only in Spanish but also in its original language and would have understood it well.[15]

When one takes Olin's interpretation and conjoins it with the fact that Ignatius composed the Principle and Foundation of the *Spiritual Exercises* during the time of his study in Paris from 1528–35, it seems plausible to assert that Ignatius did indeed read Erasmus's *Enchiridion* and interpreted Erasmus's description of an appropriate attitude one should have in regard to created things and adapted it to the Principle and Foundation in the *Spiritual*

14. In Ignatius Loyola, *Exercitia Spiritualia*, 56.

15. Olin, "Erasmus and St. Ignatius of Loyola," 77–78.

Exercises.[16] For example, in the Principle and Foundation, Ignatius, first, indicates the reason for the creation of human beings, that they are created to praise, reverence, and serve God, and by means of this, to save their souls. This is the purpose of human life. Other created things are meant to help human beings to attain their salvation (*SpEx* 23:2–3). The rest of the Principle and Foundation indicates the attitude one must have toward created things. It runs as follows:

> From this it follows that we ought to use these things to the extent that they help us toward our end, and free ourselves from them to the extent that they hinder us from it. To attain this it is necessary to make ourselves *indifferent* to all created things, in regard to everything which is left to our free will and is not forbidden. Consequently, on our own part we ought not to seek health rather than sickness, wealth rather than poverty, honor rather than dishonor, a long life rather than a short one, and so on in all other matters. Rather, we ought to desire and choose only that which is more conducive to the end for which we are created. (*SpEx* 23: 4–7) [emphasis added]

In the *Enchiridion*, particularly in the *Fourth Rule* on the following of Christ, Erasmus does not begin with the destiny of human beings, but he situates that destiny in the choosing and following of Christ. Furthermore, Erasmus does not use the word "indifferent" to describe an appropriate attitude toward created things, as Ignatius does. But his description of the appropriate attitude one should have toward wealth, poverty, health, sickness, and similar things, in relation to the choosing of Christ, originates in the same underlying principle as that propounded by Ignatius in the Principle and Foundation, as it can be observed in the passage taken from the *Fourth Rule* of the *Enchiridion*:

> Therefore, whatever you encounter on the road [in the following of Christ] as you press forward toward the goal

16. In the *Spiritual Exercises* of Saint Ignatius, the Principle and Foundation is presented as the first consideration of the purpose of God's creation, particularly the creation of human beings and the right use of created reality.

of the supreme Good, you must reject or accept solely to
the extent that it either hinders or helps your journey.
In general, these contingencies may be grouped in three
categories:

Some things—avenging an injury, for example, or
bearing malice toward another man are so abominable
that they can never be honorable. These actions or conditions you must always spurn, no matter what suffering or
exertion you incur in doing so, for nothing whatever can
harm a good man except his own vile practices.

At another extreme are certain qualities so inherently fine that they cannot be culpable, such as wishing
everyone well, helping one's friends by honorable means,
hating evil, taking pleasure in edifying conversation.

And something—health, good looks, energy,
eloquence, learning, and the like—occupy the neutral
ground. Of this last category, therefore, one should pursue none for its own sake, nor should he rely upon them
more or less than they help him hit the final mark.[17]

One observes a similar characteristic in both Erasmus and
Ignatius with regard to created things and states of lives, that they
are not constitutive to the choosing and following Christ. The
constitutive elements in the choice to follow Christ consist of only
those things that are either so bad that one must always avoid, or
so inherently good that one must always choose. Anything that
belong to the middle ground, such as riches or poverty, health or
sickness, honor or contempt, long or short life, ought to be treated
as "neutral" things. For this reason, Erasmus advises the followers
of Christ that "Whatever you encounter on the road as you press
forward toward the goal of the supreme Good, you must reject
or accept solely to the extent that it either hinders or helps your
journey."[18]

This understanding of indifference has its origin in the Stoic
philosophical tradition. Stoics use the Greek compound word *a*
(not) and *diaphoros* (different) to describe the state of indifference.

17. Himelick, trans., *The Enchiridion of Erasmus*, 95–96.
18. Ibid., 95.

Hence the combination of the prefix *a* and the adjective *diaphoros* produces *adiaphoros*, which is translated into English as "indifferent." Stoics use this term in their moral and ethical writings. They hold that one must not be indifferent to virtue and vice; that is, virtue is to be sought and vice avoided. But one should be indifferent in regard to other things, be they material things, states of life, or life circumstances.[19] In this view, wealth or poverty, health or sickness, life or death, misfortune or luck, are considered "things indifferent," not in the sense that they are not relevant or valuable, but that they are not constitutive of one's moral character. The adjective *adiaphoros* means "making no distinction," or "without discrimination," and connotes a state of being unwaveringly and steadfastly indifferent regarding things that are not constitutive of virtue and vice.[20]

Both Erasmus and Ignatius employ this understanding of indifference in their spiritual writings to signify a correct attitude toward the external factors of life that are not necessary for choosing and following Christ. Neither of them use the word "indifferent" to mean "disinterested" or "careless" in regard to the external things that are disposed to their use in the following of Christ. In their view, one ought to choose Christ as the absolute and ultimate value in life. Other things are chosen in so far as they help one to attain the choosing of Christ. Thus, to be "neutral" or "indifferent" to created things in this context means to be free of disordered attachments to them so that one can choose them for the purpose of the flourishing of one's commitment to Christ in the world.

The uniqueness of Ignatius, as compared to the Stoics' use of the word *adiaphoros*, can be seen in the way he grounds the understanding of indifference in God's love for the individual human person. In the Principle and Foundation, the state of being indifferent to created things is perceived from the ground of God's love. Here "indifference," with regard to created things, does not mean "careless," "unconcerned," or "regarding them as unimportant,"[21]

---

19. Reese, *Dictionary of Philosophy & Religion*, 335.

20. Liddell & Scott, *Greek-English Lexicon*, 22–23.

21. Ganss, *The Spiritual Exercises* of Saint Ignatius, 151n20.

as the English word "indifferent" often connotes. Rather, people can only be indifferent to created things if they have realized God's love for them. The more they become aware of the depth of God's love for them, the more they come to understand and discern their proper relation to created things, because the end—God's love and a person's response to that love—determines the means, which are God's created things. Philip Sheldrake comments on the Ignatian state of indifference in relation to created things in the followings:

> Indifference and attachment is not the first movement. Awareness of God's love and faithfulness precedes response just as the father's love was already active in the pig-sty drawing the Prodigal Son home. Put another way, we cannot become detached unless we are more and more attached to something, someone else. God draws us out of ourselves by revealing himself to us. Hence the importance of that "interior knowledge" of which Ignatius speaks. We come to love and trust the person we know. True love, built on true knowledge, enables us to allow the other to be himself. This is true of all relationships. And we have to let God be God; to let the Spirit expose our idols.[22]

In other words, Ignatius wants the retreatant to come to the realization that God wants to set him free of his disordered attachments, so that he may know God's love and respond to that love in the service of others with as much interior freedom as possible.[23] Ignatian indifference to created things really ought to be perceived in the light of God's love because only when one loves God more than any created things can one be detached from them.[24] It is because a person has realized that God loved her first that she is able to love of God in return. Her love for God manifested in the love and service of others is a response that flows from the indebtedness to God's initial love, as Saint John says in his first letter, "We

22. Sheldrake, "The Principle and Foundation and Images of God," 91.

23. Tetlow, "The Fundamentum: Creation in the Principle and Foundation," 27.

24. Emonet, "Indiferencia," 1490.

love because he first loved us" (1 John 4:19). It is this feeling of indebtedness to God's love that enables the person to be free from the disordered attachment to created things.

Ignatian *indifferentia* can be fruitfully compared to the *apatheia* discussed in the previous chapters. As already noted, Ignatius does not use the Greek word *apatheia* to describe the state of the soul in tranquility; he uses the word *indifferentia* instead. And although the two terms do not denote the same meaning, they have the same aim in that they both signify the condition of the human soul freed of disordered attachments to created reality. We find a similar ascetical method for the uprooting of the *passions* and the achieving of *apatheia* in the early church as we see in the Ignatian method for ridding ourselves of *disordered attachments* and achieving the state of *indifference*. This similarity can be observed from Ignatius's description of the purpose of the *Spiritual Exercises*, where he states, "Just as taking a walk, traveling on foot, and running are physical exercises, so is the name of spiritual exercises given to any means of presenting and disposing our soul *to rid itself of all its disordered affections* and then, after their removal, of *seeking and finding God's will* in the ordering of our life for the salvation of our soul" (*SpEx* 1:3–4 [emphasis added]).

From Ignatius's description one sees a twofold purpose of the *Spiritual Exercises*: to uproot the disordered desires in the soul and to discover the will of God for the retreatant. Though the use of language differs, Ignatius shares the traditional view on spiritual practice and divine union articulated by Evagrius Ponticus, John Cassian, and Maximus the Confessor discussed in previous chapters. These earlier theologians, though differing from each other, share one common characteristic regarding the state of *apatheia* in that they all agree that *apatheia* is the state of the tranquility of the soul, free of disordered affections to created things, a concept originating with the Stoics. Further, they perceive *apatheia* as the necessary condition for prayer and spiritual growth, without which divine union cannot be attained. Similarly, in the discovering of the will of God for the individual, Ignatius understands divine union in terms of the union of the human will to the will of God, a union that cannot be achieved unless the person's disordered affections for created reality are eradicated by means of the various exercises with the aim to attain the state of *indifferentia* (indifference).

Furthermore, as discussed in the previous chapters, Evagrius Ponticus in the fourth century developed three distinctive but interrelated stages in spiritual practice, known as *practical, natural,* and *theological* stages. These stages are progressively developed from lower to higher levels of comprehension of spiritual reality. Maximus the Confessor in the seventh century took this development from Evagrius and interpreted it for his own spiritual theology. In the Middle Ages of the Latin West, spiritual theologians inherited this tradition from the East and developed it according to their context and called the three stages the *purgative, illuminative,* and *unitive* stages. Ignatius was aware of this spiritual development in the tradition of the church. However, the *Spiritual Exercises* of Ignatius is not structured according to three progressive stages; rather, it is divided into four weeks respectively; each weak with a particular focus: the first week on sins and God's love, the second week on the contemplation of Jesus Christ and the choice to follow Christ, the third week on the passion of Christ, and the fourth week on the resurrection of Christ. Nevertheless, within the structure of the four weeks of the *Spiritual Exercises*, one can observe a similar pattern of the three stages of spiritual development. In fact, this observation has already been made by the early Jesuits and is recorded in the Official Directory of 1599. According to the early Jesuits' observation, the first week of the *Spiritual Exercises* can be compared to the *purgative* stage; the second and third weeks can be compared to the *illuminative* stage; and the fourth week can be compared to the *unitive* stage.[25]

As noted, in both Ignatius and the early theologians we have discussed in the previous chapters, the central concern of the first stage of spiritual development, the *purgative* stage, is the freedom of the soul from disordered affections to created things and the

---

25. See the "Official Directory of 1599" in Martin Palmer, trans., *On Giving the Spiritual Exercises*, no. 272–79, pp. 346–48.

cultivation of virtues. This freedom results in the stage of *apatheia* (in the early tradition) or *indifferentia* (in Ignatius). The effective method used in this first stage of spiritual development is described in both the early theologians and in Ignatius as the "technique of opposition," or in Latin, *agere contra*. In this context, the contemplative (or the retreatant in the Ignatian tradition) is encouraged to apply a corresponding virtue as a weapon to fight against his or her tendency toward a particular passion, or disordered attachment. For example, humility can be used against pride; moderation can be used against gluttony, and similarly in other passions and their corresponding virtues. Ignatius employs the same method in the *Spiritual Exercises*. For example, in *annotation* 16, Ignatius employs a method of *agere contra* and advises that if the retreatant has a disordered tendency toward riches, honor, and pride, he or she should make every possible effort to oppose this tendency, so that his or her goal becomes transparent, namely, to love and serve God in loving and serving the poor, the marginalized, and the humiliated. This advice should be interpreted in relation to the directive in *annotation* 15, where Ignatius insists that the discovering of God's will for the individual is the work of grace, and thus, it is more appropriate that God communicates this will directly to the retreatant.[26]

The implication in these two *annotations* is twofold. First, similar to the first stage in spiritual practice in the early church tradition, a retreatant is encouraged to make an effort to fight against his or her tendency toward the vices and to develop the corresponding virtues. Second, the director (a person who guides the retreatant) should also maintain a state of indifference with regard to the direction in which the Holy Spirit is moving in the retreatant; that is, the director should not incline toward one way or another based on his or her opinions and biases, but should remain in equilibrium and let God deal immediately with the

26. Before the actual text of the *Spiritual Exercises*, Ignatius composes twenty *annotations*. These are preliminary explanations to the *Spiritual Exercises*. For the complete text of *annotations* 15 and 16, see Ganss's translation of the *Spiritual Exercises* of Saint Ignatius, pp. 25–26.

retreatant. The twofold implication here is pivotal in understanding how the Ignatian indifference works. On the one hand, it is *God* who is actively at work in the human soul during the retreat bringing about the state of indifference in the person, and this results in the retreatant's self-realization of God's love for her. The director does not direct the retreatant; *God* does. For this reason, the director, too ought to maintain the state of indifference in regard to the interior direction in which the retreatant is moving. But on the other hand, the director's role is crucial in the guiding of the retreatant during the retreat. He should be an active participant in the movements of the retreatant's spirit, but best as a listener and an observer of the retreatant's spiritual movements, not as the director of the movements. The director observes the movements of retreatant's spirit and gives advice when needed. But he ought to entrust to God the outcome of the retreat.

As already discussed, although Ignatius does not structure the *Spiritual Exercises* according to the three distinctive movements of the early tradition, there can be observed the same three progressive stages of spiritual development in the *Spiritual Exercises*. The first moment is expressed in the Principle and Foundation, as already discussed. The second moment begins with the exercises on the Call of Christ the King in the second week of the *Spiritual Exercises*. It is here in the exercises on the Call of Christ the King, particularly in the presentation on the Three Types of Human Beings, that Ignatius makes use for the second time the term "indifferent" (*SpEx* 157).

To elicit the retreatant's desire to choose Christ in the world instead of choosing the value-system of the world, which competes with the gospel of Christ, Ignatius describes two contrasting value-systems embraced by two imaginative kings, one by Lucifer, the other by Christ. Those who follow Lucifer are promised with riches, honor, and pride; whereas, those who follow Jesus Christ will take on poverty, humiliation, and humility as their standard of life (*SpEx*, 142, 146). One observes again the employment of the "technique of opposition" here. In order to fight against the tendency toward riches, honor, and pride proposed by Lucifer,

Ignatius recommends that one embraces poverty, humiliation, and humility as the counter-standard. It is important to underscore again that for Ignatius, riches, honor, and pride are not bad in and of themselves, but they are not constitutive of one's desire to follow Christ, and thus one should maintain a state of indifference toward them.

To achieve this indifference, Ignatius categorize people into three different types. People who belong to the first type are the people who seem to have the desire to follow Christ, but they do not want to make the necessary changes in their life in order to follow him. The second type of people desire to follow Christ, but would do so on their own terms; that is, they want to make the necessary changes in their life in order to follow Christ, but would do so according to what they want. Finally, people who belong to the third type want to follow Christ and wish to do so in ways that God inspires them (*SpEx* 153–155).[27] The difference among the three types of people signifies the various levels of indifference regarding created things, states of life, and life circumstances that corresponding to three different levels of spiritual freedom in their desire to follow Christ. Ignatius perceives the third type to be the most desirable in the following of Christ, not because the people belonging to third type love created things any less than those belonging to the first two types, but because their love for God in Christ affects their choices in life. God's love enables them to possess a higher degree of spiritual freedom in the pursuit of Christ and to make choices that are more conducive to their responses to God's love in Christ.[28] As mentioned, it is here in the exercises on the Three Types of People that Ignatius advises those who find themselves challenged by the standard of Christ to ask for the grace to embrace poverty. The most effective way to overcome one's disordered attachment to riches, in Ignatius view, is to beg God for the grace to embrace actual poverty as a counteraction against riches (*SpEx* 157).

---

27. Barry, *Finding God in All Things*, 108–9.

28. Ivens, *Understanding the Spiritual Exercises*, 118.

Then Ignatius presents the Three Degrees of Humility corresponding to the Three Types of people discussed above. The first degree of humility manifests in those who want to follow Christ merely by observing the ten commandments so as to not commit sin (*SpEx* 165). The second degree manifests a higher desire in the person in the following of Christ. He or she does not want to stop short at the observance of the commandments, but wants to do God's will as he or she understands it. The third degree includes the first and second degrees of humility. People who embrace this degree of humility desire Christ for *his* sake, rather than for their sake. Ignatius describes the proper attitude of those who embrace the third degree of humility as follows: "I want to choose poverty with Christ poor rather than wealth, and humiliations with Christ humiliated rather than fame, and I desire more to be thought worthless and a fool for Christ, who first was taken to be such, rather than to be esteemed as wise and prudent in this world" (*SpEx* 167). Similar to the third type of people who embrace actual poverty discussed above, humility and contempt are embraced as forms of spiritual poverty; they are effective weapons against riches, honor, and pride. People who embrace the third degree of humility want to put on Christ's self-emptying as their own, a kind of self-emptying described by Saint Paul in Philippians 2:6–8 when he says that although Christ was in the form of God, he humbled himself in becoming human, to suffer and even die on the cross.

Ignatian scholars have commented on the relation among the three degrees of humility. Michael Ivens, for example, observes that the three degrees of humility serve to help people to check their dispositions regarding their choices in the following of Christ. The first kind is required but not sufficient to attain the necessary disposition. The second is sufficient and required. The third is not only sufficient and required, but also desirable. Eliás Royón perceives the difference between the second and third kinds of humility not only in terms of degrees, but of perspectives. He asserts that the second degree of humility is to exemplify *indifferentia* as you embrace the state of life you understand to be God's will for you. Whereas, in the third degree, you not only choose what God wants for you personally, but consciously and intentionally choose to identify with the humble, poor, and humiliated God in Christ.[29] Ivens, however, cautions that not everyone will attain the same degree of disposition to do the will of God in the following of Christ. Here Iven shares the view of Thomas Aquinas, who said, "What is received is received according to the mode of the one receiving."[30] In an ultimate sense, the degree of disposition one has in the following of Christ is perceived as a gift from God which should be proper to one's personal characteristics and traits.

The second week of the *Spiritual Exercises* of Saint Ignatius—particularly in the exercises on the Call of Christ the King, which is culminated in the exercises in the Election—shares the characteristic of the second stage of spiritual development in the early church tradition discussed in the previous chapters. In the early church tradition, the second way, the *illuminative* way, is built on the first way, the *purgative* way, with an emphasis on the contemplation of God in created reality. Ignatius does not present the exercises on the Call of Christ the King and on the Election in the traditional way, but by having the retreatant imagine Christ and his standard in contradistinction to that of Lucifer, and in eliciting the desire to disdain the latter while to choose the former, Ignatius helps the retreatant to see God in Christ and to make a choice to follow Christ. This enlightening process can be compared to the *illuminative* way in the early tradition presented by Evagrius and Maximus. Just as Evagrius and Maximus perceived the passions as potential hindrances in the spiritual development of a contemplative—in that they prevent him or her from seeing the essence of created things as intrinsically good—so too Ignatius conceives the potential danger generated in the person's disordered attachments to riches, honor, and pride. For Ignatius, these attachments impede the process of growth in the spiritual life of the person and disrupt the person's desire to following Christ in the world.

The distinctive characteristic of the *Spiritual Exercises* of Saint Ignatius can be seen in the final stage of spiritual development, the

29. Royón, "Principio y Fundamento," 1494–96.
30. Ivens, *Understanding the Spiritual Exercises*, 123–24.

unitive stage. Javier Melloni correctly observes that the Ignatian name for divine union is "Election," which we have previously discussed. But the Ignatian Election is not a definitive state, as was in the early tradition, particularly as it was in the view of Evagrius. Rather, the Ignatian Election presents a quest and a tendency that requires an ongoing discernment of God's will.[31] The ultimate goal of the *Spiritual Exercises* of Saint Ignatius, like that of the early tradition, is divine union. But for Ignatius, this divine union is expressed in the final consideration of the *Spiritual Exercises*, known as the Contemplation to Attain Love, whereby Ignatius insists that love ought to manifest itself in deeds more than in words (*SpEx* 230). The Ignatian divine union is perceived as a *union-in-action*; that is, a union in a life of service, commonly known as *contemplation-in-action*.

To conceive how this union is possible, one should see how the Contemplation to Attain Love relates to the rest of the *Spiritual Exercises*. In the exercises on the Contemplation to Attain Love, Ignatius does not use the word "indifferent." But the state of indifference to created things, states of life, and life circumstances discussed in the previous exercises is presupposed. In fact, without the attitude of indifference attained in the previous exercises, it is not possible for the retreatant to consider the Contemplation to Attain Love at the end of the *Spiritual Exercises*. Ivens has effectively described the essential relationship between the Contemplation to Attain Love and the Principle and Foundation (the first consideration of the *Spiritual Exercises*) as follows:

> The Principle and Foundation emphasizes more our dependency on God, while the Contemplation to Attain Love puts greater stress on God's gift of himself to us. In the Principle and Foundation, we use creatures to relate to God, in the Contemplation to Attain Love God uses his creation to give himself to us. The Principle and Foundation calls forth primarily the response of service, the Contemplation to Attain Love that of gratitude. In

31. Melloni, *The Exercises of St. Ignatius Loyola in the Western Tradition*, 50.

the Principle and Foundation, the concrete conditions of service (right use and indifference) are presented as a task or as objectives to be achieved, while the self-offering of the Contemplation to Attain Love is presented as lovingly spontaneous. In brief, it could be said that the emphases of Principle and Foundation are preparatory to those of the Contemplation to Attain Love, and essential to the authenticity of the latter. The two texts however are mutually complementary, each dealing with the themes of God's creative purpose and of the place of humankind within that purpose.[32]

Thus, the Principle and Foundation (the first consideration in the *Spiritual Exercises*) is perceived as the necessary condition for the Contemplation to Attain Love (the final consideration in the *Spiritual Exercises*) without which the divine union proposed in the Contemplation to Attain Love cannot be realized. Conversely, the Contemplation to Attain Love is perceived as the final end of the *Spiritual Exercises*, which is the union between the individual human will and the will of God, a union that, once achieved, makes possible the living out of the Principle and Foundation spontaneously. The difference between the Principle and Foundation and the Contemplation to Attain Love is one of perspective: in the Principle and Foundation one is advised to rightly choose God's creation for the purpose of serving God and others; whereas, in the Contemplation to Attain Love, as one has been completely disposed to the will of God, God can use you to give life to creation. One becomes God's agent of grace to the world.[33]

The Contemplation to Attain Love is the continuation of the exercises on the Call of Christ the King and is intrinsically related to them. As already discussed, in the exercise on the Call of Christ the King, Ignatius presents the two standards—one of Christ and one of Lucifer—with the aim of eliciting in the retreatant the desire to follow Christ and his value system. The culmination of this process is expressed in the Election, as we have seen. But it does

32. Ivens, *Understanding the Spiritual Exercises*, 26n13.
33. Royón, "Principio y Fundamento," 1492.

not stop there. Rather, it continues into the third and fourth weeks of the *Spiritual Exercises* and comes to its climatic moment in the final consideration described in the Contemplation to Attain Love.

Theologically Ignatius makes a shift in the Christological focus in the Contemplation to Attain Love. The retreatant is invited to see how the divinity of Christ is both present and at work in creation (*SpEx* 235–36). Christ's humanity is not absent in the retreatant's consideration of Contemplation to Attain Love, but the retreatant has now been transformed by Christ's divinity, and thus is able to see the world from the divine influence, which makes it possible for God to work in and through him or her. As noted, the Directory of 1599 conceives the Ignatian Contemplation to Attain Love as belonging to the *unitive* way (Directory of 1599, 43:253). But seen from the perspective of Contemplative in Action, the Ignatian *unitive* way signifies a unique development that departs from the *unitive* way conceived in the early tradition: while Ignatius shares with the early tradition the distinctive characteristic of the *unitive* way in that divine union signifies the work of grace and the utter disposition of the person to God's grace, in the case of the Ignatian Contemplation to Attain Love, this characteristic manifests itself in *action*; that is, it manifests itself in the person's life of service of others, especially in the service of those who are in need of God's love. Election, the Ignatian term for divine union, is a *dynamic* relationship between God and the human person that requires continual discernment of spirits on the part of the person in the discovering of God's will and in doing that will as he or she follows Christ in the world. This dynamic relationship, though it reaches its climax in the Contemplation to Attain Love, does not become static, but continues to generate the divine energy in the person, and through him or her pours out that energy to the world. In so far as you are conscious of God's grace operating on you and are intentional about cooperating with God's grace in your choice and action, God can act in and through you spontaneously because you are utterly immersed in the mystery of God and effortlessly surrender to God's will.

This chapter has underscored the common characteristic shared by Ignatian "indifference" and the early tradition's *apatheia* in that both terms signified the state of the soul in tranquility, free of disordered attachments. The distinctive development in Ignatius was articulated from his view on the final stage of spiritual practice, the *unitive* stage. Ignatius saw this is a *dynamic* state in which the person's union with God manifested itself in an active life of serving God through serving others, as opposed to the static state of divine union conceived by Evagrius Ponticus in the early tradition. The Ignatian divine union, therefore, is best described as a contemplation-in-action, a state of life possible only if one has achieved the state of indifference to created reality.

Conclusion

We have explored the nature and function of *apatheia* in the Christian spiritual tradition by tracing its root to the Stoics. In doing so, I argued that the Stoic *apatheia* is not a non-emotional state, as it is often perceived, but it is a state of the soul in tranquility, free of excessive emotions, such as lust, greed, anger, envy, boredom, and pride.

The Stoics perceived excessive emotions as various forms of the sickness of the soul, and they invented a method for uprooting these excessive emotions. The key insight offered by the Stoics was that emotions were mental judgments and attitudes toward the factors of life. But when emotions became excessive, their judgments became distorted, and thus needed to be eradicated. The process of eradicating the excessive emotions consisted of an education that aimed to cultivate a correct knowledge of the relation between the factors of life and our judgments of them. This was coupled with a method for spiritual practice that aimed to cultivate virtues. Thus, knowledge and virtues were considered the necessary condition for a happy life.

Early church theologians interpreted the Stoic insight on excessive emotions and *apatheia* for their own spiritual theology and developed a prayer method aimed at countering excessive emotions and attaining the state of *apatheia*. They called the Stoics' "excessive emotions" the "passions," and described these passions as "unnatural movements of the soul." Ignatius of Loyola in the sixteenth century called these same unnatural movements of the soul "disordered affections." In this sense, both "passion" and "disordered affection" signified the contrary state to *apatheia*.

From a spiritual point of view, when a person is experiencing one or more of the passions, it is impossible for her or him to pray. Thus, the first step in prayer is to prepare the soul for prayer by uprooting any passion one may have experienced and thereby cultivating virtues. When the passions are removed, the soul can perceive the nature of created reality in its own essence. It is like a mirror that has been cleaned of dust, enabling one to see the objects in the mirror with clarity. This comes as the result of the second stage of prayer, which the early church called *natural contemplation* or the *illuminative way*, and corresponds to the second and third weeks of the *Spiritual Exercises* of Saint Ignatius. The final stage of prayer leads to divine union. This final state is the work of God's grace, but it is also conditioned by the human efforts in preparing the soul in the first two stages.

Ignatius of Loyola lived many centuries after the first three theologians discussed in this book, yet he is clearly developing a tradition of spiritual transformation inherited from them. In the *Spiritual Exercises*, Ignatius presented the concept of *indifferentia* as the necessary condition for the person's choice to follow Jesus Christ in the world. Though *indifferentia* and *apatheia* are different words, and have different connotations, nonetheless, from the point of view of spiritual practice, they signify the same condition of the soul in tranquility, free of disordered affections to created reality, as a necessary condition for prayer and spiritual growth.

We have examined various views on *apatheia* and *indifferentia* and the different theological anthropologies underpinning them. It became clear that any theological anthropology that is grounded on a dualistic tendency is in danger of ending up with an unhealthy spiritual practice. This was seen in Evagrius Ponticus, who conceived of *apatheia* as the *total eradication* of emotion, rather than the purification and right ordering of emotion. In this, Evagrius was unintentionally moving away from Christian theological insights. In orthodox Christian faith, it is believed that God was incarnated in Jesus Christ, becoming fully human (John 1:14), and thus, the material world and the human body are perceived as *intrinsically good* because they are created by God. Thus, contra Evagrius, it is not emotion that is bad, but *disordered* emotion (which the tradition called "passions"). A more biblical theological anthropology, which corrected Evagrius's misstep here while seeking to preserve his genuine insights, was presented and argued for by John Cassian, Maximus the Confessor, and Ignatius of Loyola.

Every human being has a desire to be united with the divine. In the Christian tradition, prayer lies at the heart of that desire. But the questions arise: How does one pray? What is the purpose of prayer? What is the underpinning theological anthropology on which one articulates the theology of prayer? This short book has sought to take a few steps toward answering these questions, and in doing so, I pray, to assist readers in some way on their own spiritual journey.

APPENDIX

Apatheia in the Spiritual Life

	Stoics	Evagrius	John Cassian	Maximus	Ignatius
Anthropology	Human beings are endowed with reason and intellectual will suitable for a life in pursuit of knowledge and virtue.	Human beings are created in the image and likeness of God and thus, inherit a desire for divine union and are capable of it.	Human beings are created in the image and likeness of God and thus, inherit a desire for divine union and are capable of it.	Human beings are created in the image and likeness of God and thus, inherit a desire for divine union and are capable of it.	The end of human life is to know, love, and serve God. All created things are considered the means to this end.

	Stoics	Evagrius	John Cassian	Maximus	Ignatius
Apatheia	The healthy state of the soul, whereby the soul is free of excessive emotions, while healthy emotions remain.	The state of the soul free of the eight passions: gluttony, lust, greed, envy, anger, boredom, self-love, and pride. These "passions" are defined as "unnatural movements of the soul." *Apatheia* signifies the state of the mind independent of the bodily senses. Prayer is the state of *mind*.	The Greek term *apatheia* is replaced by the Latin term *puritas cordis* (purity of heart) to signify a heart that is free of the eight passions: gluttony, lust, greed, envy, anger, boredom, self-love, and pride, and to emphasize that prayer is the movement of the *heart* rather than the knowledge gained by the mind.	The state of the soul free of the eight passions: gluttony, lust, greed, envy, anger, boredom, self-love, and pride. These "passions" are defined as the "unnatural movements of the soul." *Apatheia* signifies the state of the soul whereby the passions are transformed into *agape* (a non-egoistic love).	The term *indifferentia* (indifference) signifies the state of the soul free of "disordered affections" for created reality, whereby "disordered affections" are comparable to the "passions" in the early church tradition.

	Stoics	Evagrius	John Cassian	Maximus	Ignatius
Stage I	The "technique of opposition" is applied. Example: *joy, caution,* and *wish* are used to counter *distress,* excessive *pleasure,* excessive *fear,* and excessive *desire*	*Practical* stage: The "technique of opposition" is applied by using one virtue to fight against a particular passion, for example, humility against pride; moderate intake of food and drink against gluttony.	There are no distinguished stages of prayer. The method of *agere contra* (to go against) is applied, for example, humility against pride; moderate intake of food and drink against gluttony. Put more emphasis on the importance of attaining the stage of good intention of the heart more than on the mind's capacity for prayer. The final aim of prayer is to purge the ill intention of the heart. Divine union takes place in the heart rather than in the mind.	*Practical* stage: The goal is to transform the passions and to cultivate virtues. The "technique of opposition" is applied in the similar way as compared to Evagrius Ponticus and John Cassian	Week 1: Contemplating on the history of sin, both personal and social sins and on God's love and mercy in forgiving sins. The retreatant experiences that he/she is a sinner, but loved by God. This experience stirs in the retreatant a sense of gratitude for God's love and the desire to follow Jesus Christ to serve God. The first week can be compared to the *practical* stage (or *purgative way*) in the early church tradition.

	Stoics	Evagrius	John Cassian	Maximus	Ignatius
Stage 2	Cultivating correct mental judgment and attitude toward external factors of life	*Nature* stage: The mind is advanced and capable to know created things for what they truly are and to see God through them.		*Natural* stage: The mind is advanced in prayer and capable to know created things for what they truly are and to see God through them.	Weeks 2 & 3: Focus on Jesus Christ's vision and value-system, which is contrary to the vision and value-system of Lucifer, the enemy of human nature. The retreatant makes a choice to follow Jesus Christ by living Christ's vision and value-system while refusing those of Lucifer. The retreatant's choice is tested and affirmed in the contemplation on the passion and death of Jesus, whereby the

	Stoics	Evagrius	John Cassian	Maximus	Ignatius
					retreatant deepens his/her choice to serve God in serving the poor, the marginalized, and the neglected of the world. Weeks 2 & 3 can be compared to the *natural* stage (or *illuminative* stage) in the early church tradition.

	Stoics	Evagrius	John Cassian	Maximus	Ignatius
Stage 3	Attaining the stage of the soul in tranquility, free of excessive emotions and in which only joy, caution, and wish remain	*Theological* stage: The mind is able to contemplate God in an immaterial manner, independent of the mediation of the senses. Divine union is perceived as a static state of the soul in union with God.		*Theological* stage: The passions are transformed into *agape* (non-egoistic love). Divine union is perceived not as a static but dynamic state of the soul in union with God.	Week 4: The retreatant contemplates on the resurrection of Jesus as a victory over sin and death, whereby he/she understands that suffering can be transformed into love, and death can be transformed into life. The Contemplation to Attain Love (the final contemplation in the *Spiritual Exercises*) can be compared to the *theological* stage (or *unitive* stage) in the early church, but with a distinctive emphasis: the

Stoics	Evagrius	John Cassian	Maximus	Ignatius
				retreatant is inspired to love God in working to bring about peace and justice in the world. This is called *Contemplative in Action*.

Bibliography

Annas, Julie. *An Introduction to Plato's Republic*. Oxford: Clarendon, 1981.

Balthasar, Hans Urs von. *Cosmic Liturgy: The Universe according to Maximus the Confessor*. San Francisco: Ignatius, 2003.

Barry, William A. *Finding God in All Things: A Companion to the Spiritual Exercises of St. Ignatius*. Notre Dame, IN: Ave Maria, 1991.

Blowers, Paul M., "Gentiles of the Soul: Maximus the Confessor on the Substructure and Transformation of the Human Passions." *Journal of Early Christian Studies* vol. 4, no. 1 (1996) 57–85.

Cattoi, Thomas. "An Evagrian *Hypostasis*? Leontios of Byzantium and the 'Composite Subjectivity' of the Person of Christ." In *Studia Patristica*, vol. LXVIII, edited by Markus Vinzent, 133–47. Leuven: Peeters, 2013.

Conway, Charles Abbott. *The Vita Christi of Ludolph of Saxony and Late Medieval Devotion Centered on the Incarnation: A Descriptive Analysis*. Analecta Cartusiana. Salzburg: University of Salzburg, 1976.

Cunningham, Lawrence S. "Cassian's Hero and Discernment." In *Finding God in All Things: Essays in Honor of Michael J. Buckley, S.J.*, edited by Michael J. Himes and Stephen J. Pope, 231–43. New York: Crossroad, 1996.

De Dalmases, Cándido. *Ignatius of Loyola, Founder of the Jesuits: His Life and Work*. Translated by Jerome Aixalá. Saint Louis: The Institute of Jesuit Sources, 1985.

Davis, Leo Donald. *The First Seven Ecumenical Council (325–787): Their History and Theology*. Collegeville, MN: Liturgical, 1990.

Divarkar, Parmananda R., trans. *The Pilgrim's Testament: The Memoirs of St. Ignatius of Loyola*. Saint Louis: The Institute of Jesuit Sources, 1995.

Driscoll, Jeremy. *Steps to Spiritual Perfection: Studies on Spiritual Progress in Evagrius Ponticus*. Mahwah, NJ: Newman, 2005.

Emonet, Pierre. "Indiferencia." In *Diccionario de Espiritualidad Ignaciana*, edited by José García de Castro, 1015–21. Mensajero: Sal Terrae, 2007.

Feldmeier, Peter. *Christian Spirituality: Lived Expressions in the Life of the Church*. Winona, MN: Anselm Academic, 2015.

Ganss, George E., trans. *The Spiritual Exercises of Saint Ignatius*. Saint Louis: The Institute of the Jesuit Sources, 1992.

Bibliography

Greer, Rowan A., trans. *Origen: Selected Writings. (An Exhortation to Martyrdom, Prayer, First Principles: Book IV, Prologue to the Commentary on the Song of Songs, Homily XXVII on Numbers.)* The Classics of Western Spirituality. New York: Paulist, 1979.

Hadot, Pierre. *Philosophy as a Way of Life: Spiritual Exercises from Socrates to Foucault.* Translated by Michael Chase. Malden, MA: Blackwell, 1995.

Harmless, William. *Desert Christians.* Oxford: Oxford University Press, 2004.

Harmless, William, and Raymond Fitzgerald, trans. "The Sapphire Light of the Mind: The *Skemmata* of Evagrius Ponticus." *Theological Studies,* vol. 62, no. 3 (2001) 493–529.

Healey, Charles J. "The Imitation of Christ Revisited." In *The Best of the Review: Notes on the Spiritual Exercises of St. Ignatius of Loyola,* vol. 1, edited by David L. Fleming, 126–33. Saint Louis: Review for Religious, 1983.

Himelick, Raymond, trans. *The Enchiridion of Erasmus.* Bloomington, IN: Indiana University Press, 1963.

Ignatius Loyola. *Exercitia Spiritualia: Textuum Antiquissimorum Nova Editio Lexicon Textus Hispani.* Opus Inchoavit Iosephus Calveras, obsolvit Candidus de Dalmases. Rome: Institutum Historicum Societatis Iesu, 1969.

Inwood, Brad, and Lloyd P. Gerson, trans. *The Stoics Reader: Selected Writing and Testimonia.* Indianapolis: Hackett, 2008.

Ivens, Michael. *Understanding the Spiritual Exercises.* Leominster, UK: Gracewing, 1998.

Liddell, Henry George, and Robert Scott. *Greek-English Lexicon.* Oxford: Clarendon, 1968.

Louth, Andrew. *Maximus the Confessor.* London: Routledge, 1996.

Luibheid, Colm, trans. *John Cassian: Conferences.* Classics of Western Spirituality. New York: Paulist, 1985.

Melloni, Javier. *The Exercises of St. Ignatius Loyola in the Western Tradition.* Leominster, UK: Gracewing, 2000.

Nussbaum, Martha C. *The Therapy of Desire: Theory and Practice in Hellenistic Ethics.* Princeton: Princeton University Press, 1994.

Olin, John C., "Erasmus and St. Ignatius of Loyola." In *Six Essays on Erasmus: And a Translation of Erasmus' Letter to Carondelet, 1523,* 74–92. New York: Fordham University Press, 1979.

Padberg, John, ed. *The Constitutions of the Society of Jesus and Their Complementary Norms: The Complete English Translation of the Official Latin Texts.* Saint Louis: The Institute of Jesuit Sources, 2009.

———. *Jesuit Life & Mission Today: The Decrees & Accompanying Documents of the 31st –35th General Congregations of the Society of Jesus.* Saint Louis: The Institute of Jesuit Sources, 2009.

Palmer, G. E. H., Philip Sherrard, and Kallistos Ware, trans. & eds. *The Philokalia: The Complete Text,* 4 Volumes. New York: Faber and Faber, 1979–1995.

Bibliography

Palmer, Martin E., trans. and ed. *On Giving the Spiritual Exercises: The Early Jesuit Manuscript Directories and the Official Directory of 1599*. Saint Louis: The Institute of Jesuit Sources, 1996.

Prassas, Despina D., trans. *St. Maximus the Confessor's Questions and Doubts*. DeKalb, IL: Northern Illinois University Press, 2010.

Reese, William L., *Dictionary of Philosophy & Religion: Eastern and Western Thought*. New and enlarged ed. Atlantic Highlands, NJ: Humanities, 1996.

Rist, J. M. *Stoic Philosophy*. Cambridge: Cambridge University Press, 1969.

Royón, Elías. "Principio y Fundamento." In *Diccionario de Espiritualidad Ignaciana*, edited by José García de Castro, 111–13. Mensajero: Sal Terrae, 2007.

Sheldrake, Philip. "The Principle and Foundation and Images of God." *The Way*, Supplement 48, Autumn 1983, 90–96.

Sherwood, Polycarp. trans. *St. Maximus the Confessor: The Ascetic Life and the Four Centuries on Charity*. Mahwah, NJ: Newman, 1955.

Shore, Paul. "The *Vita Christi* of Ludolph of Saxony and Its Influence on the *Spiritual Exercises* of Ignatius of Loyola." *Studies in the Spirituality of Jesuits* vol. 30, no. 1 (1998).

Sinkewwicz, Robert E., trans., *Evagrius of Ponticus: The Greek Ascetic Corpus*. Oxford: Oxford University Press, 2003.

Sorabji, Richard. *Emotion and Peace of Mind: From Stoic Agitation to Christian Temptation*. Oxford: Oxford University Press, 2000.

Stewart, Columba. *Cassian the Monk*. Oxford: Oxford University Press, 1998.

Tetlow, Joseph A. "The Fundamentum: Creation in the Principle and Foundation." *Studies in the Spirituality of Jesuits*, vol. 21, no. 4 (1989).

Thunberg, Lars. *Microcosm and Mediator: The Theological Anthropology of Maximus the Confessor*. Chicago: Open Court, 1995.

Wilken, Robert L. "Maximus the Confessor on the Affections in Historical Perspective." In *Asceticism*, edited by Vincent L. Wilmbush and Richard Valentasis, 412–23. New York: Oxford University Press, 1995.

www.ingramcontent.com/pod-product-compliance
Lightning Source LLC
Chambersburg PA
CBHW030852090426
42737CB00009B/1207